Bunny Cole

Bunny Cole
An Oxford Man

A biography of Raymond Buxton Cole
DSO TD DL MA

by

Richard Cole

The Memoir Club

First published in 2010 by
The Memoir Club
Arya House
Langley Park
Durham
DH7 9XE
0191 373 5660

British Library Cataloguing in
Publication Data.
A catalogue record for this book
is available from the
British Library

ISBN: 978-1-84104-516-0

Typeset by Words by Design, Oxford
Printed by Charlesworth Press, Wakefield

CONTENTS

LIST OF ILLUSTRATIONS

ACKNOWLEDGEMENTS

I am very grateful to family and friends alike for their help in gathering information.

My thanks go to Peter Thompson (who sadly died before publication) for his encouragement.

To Gavin Clezy for putting me in touch with Lynn Davidson and The Memoir Club. Their professional help has been invaluable.

PREFACE

This is a factual account of an amazing man who was loved and respected by many people.

The story starts with his own history of life in Oxford as the youngest son of the Chief Constable, involving the impact of the Great War upon the family.

After that war, he describes building a career as a solicitor and then when another war seemed inevitable joining the Territorial Army and later enlisting in the Royal Artillery and being posted to Burma.

There he commanded British troops in the Battle of the Admin Box which led to the first defeat of the Japanese Forces. He was awarded the DSO and presented with his ribbon in the field by Lord Louis Mountbatten.

After victory in 1945 he returned 'with a mission' to support others in the provision of sporting facilities in the Oxford area by the founding of the Oxford Sports Club. Returning to professional life, he entered into a partnership of solicitors (Cole & Cole) which became for a time one of the largest in the country.

In the meantime he led the life of a family man until his death in 1991. Bunny Cole was described by a former Lord Mayor of Oxford as being 'as much a part of Oxford as Carfax' (the main crossing in the centre of Oxford) and this is his story.

INTRODUCTION

1. Bunny with author, aged six weeks

I RETIRED ON 6 July 2007, having become the longest serving Circuit Judge in the country. At that time I had in mind that the average period of retirement for Circuit Judges until death was merely eighteen months. Whether the figures are still accurate I do not know and I am not going to waste valuable time finding out. The result of any enquiry could be depressing at the very least.

However, I realised that with advancing years it was important to keep the brain active. My initial intention was to potter about in the garden and spend a financially unhealthy period of time at the races. I realised that there were also other time hazards that I should avoid if possible, and having received three offers in the first month of my retirement to undertake voluntary jobs for the benefit of the community I knew that I ought to have an honourable reason for saying 'no'. My conscience, however, is clear, having undertaken numerous honorary jobs over the years, most of which I enjoyed although they were all time-consuming.

My father, Raymond Buxton Cole, was, I was told at an early age, a great man and a good egg and as I went through life I was in awe of him and very anxious to live up to his expectations. I frequently let him down but he persevered and gave me enormous help, as he did with family, friends and strangers alike. He was ready to help if he could and almost always did.

He was known by so many people and was called or referred to by a wide range of names, depending who and what you were. These names would include Mr R.B.; Colonel; King; Bunny; Bun or Uncle Bun, so that hereafter I shall refer to him as Bunny, although I personally would always call him Dad.

In the 1960s I had to write a very important letter, as President of The Frewen Club in Oxford. The club had an opportunity to purchase the freehold of its premises. Support for the project was by no means assured and it was important that my letter to the membership explaining the facts and urging support should hit exactly the right note. I thought that my draft letter was not too bad but I asked Bunny to have a look at it as I knew that he was extremely interested, and as he was a past President his views would carry enormous weight. When the draft was returned to me later the same day I was horrified to see that it was smothered with red ink alterations. He had not, however, destroyed my work: he had perfected it. The letter was duly sent as amended and the scheme was later approved by the membership without opposition and the purchase was completed to the permanent benefit of the club.

Upon his death, and that of my mother, Edith, I took possession of many boxes of unfiled papers and I realised that at some stage someone would have to go through them to separate the wheat from the chaff.

Inevitably to my mind, it became a job for retirement. Initially, my plan was to rescue any letters or notes of interest and to destroy the remainder but it soon became important to realise that until we had all the facts we were not going to be able to realise exactly what was important or what was going to be of interest. My sister, Rosemary, who is very good at research and detail and my brother, John, who is extremely busy, have agreed to my writing this book, and for my part I will continue to consult with them at all relevant stages in its preparation, and I hope that the finished product will be as accurate and as fair as possible.

Initially, the book is for the benefit of the family and close friends and, of course, anyone else who may wish to read it. We realise that it will not be as exciting as many modern thrillers but it is the story of a good man. Without such an account being written one feared that a life would pass away with perhaps an empty chapter.

When Bunny was alive we realised the need for an account and begged him to write his own story. To that end and perhaps on one of his retirements (and there were many) we provided him with a Dictaphone and cassettes. We realised that his mind was not as good as it had been and expected very little from that source. Fortunately, we have been able to find extensive notes of his childhood antics and the effect that the First World War had upon him as a child.

To that extent, part of the text can take the form of an autobiography and we will not have to rely, as we originally intended, upon various stories that were passed down to us as children. The reader will understand that individual chapters will be attributed to different authors as far as it is possible but as the notional author I reserve the right to interrupt when it is necessary, within my discretion. Perhaps I should add 'subject to my being overruled by the family'.

Both Oswald and Emma Cole (our grandparents) died before I was born but as parents of Bunny and others they play an important part in the story as do their many children and other offspring.

To write about sensitive matters within the family has to be done with care. In his note Bunny makes it clear that he has omitted parts of the story where there is the risk of hurt or distress being caused to others. Due to the effluxion of time perhaps there will no longer be distress, but of course we have no way of telling which matters were then excluded so the information may well also have passed away.

A number of basic rules were handed down to us as children which perhaps should be borne in mind by the reader. Sometimes we were told that it is permitted to alter facts to make a better story provided it does not mislead or cause harm or distress to others. Secondly, we were told that a joke twice repeated loses its charm. The alleged breaches of this led to many academic arguments.

Bunny was a lover of plain English and was a disciple of Sir Ernest Gower's book under that title. This book will, therefore, be written without the aid or hindrance of the sort of prose which has to be read over and over again before the reader is able to understand it – at least we hope so.

The war years, as one would expect, need special mention and have proved the most difficult to narrate for a number of reasons, particularly as the war took place over sixty years ago and Bunny died in 1991. Those who took an active part in the war will either be of very advanced years or have died. Certainly, I do not know of anyone who is still living who served with Bunny in Burma, but I hope to be proved wrong.

The other difficulty is that although we were aware that Bunny had won the DSO and, as I told my kindergarten headmistress at the time, that 'Dad had won the GPO', we hardly ever mentioned the war or Bunny's part in it and I am ashamed to say that I did not read any of the books about it until I settled down to prepare this account. My son, James, on the other hand, who had been commissioned into the Royal Green Jackets, did talk to Bunny as soldier to soldier but again that was some time ago.

Alison, my daughter, remembers being told by her grandfather that when he was in Burma it was incredibly hot and that on one occasion he was given some eggs but had no means of cooking them. He ended up frying them on the bonnet of his jeep. This was successful although the eggs tasted a bit 'gritty'.

There have, however, been a number of books written which relate to the campaign in Burma which mention Bunny specifically and to which I will later refer. I am hopeful that rather than re-write the story I will, with permission of the publishers or relatives of the authors, be able to extract portions of such available works so that I will be able to present an accurate picture of the scene and the sacrifices which were made by so many.

THE GREAT FROST

RESEARCH INTO SOMEONE ELSE'S life, albeit a relation, throws up facts which must have had considerable impact on daily life. Such an event did happen in the winter of 1895 when the temperature was so cold that the Isis froze over and a local livery stable keeper was able to drive a coach and four along the frozen river with at least ten adults on board. Some may think that this was folly indeed, bearing in mind that the total weight of horses, carriage and people was in the region of seven tons. The reason that I mention this act of madness is because my grandfather, Oswald Cole, was sitting on top of the coach.

In fact, the *Oxford Mail* records show that the river froze over in 1882, 1885, 1901, 1929 and 1947 so that it was not such a remarkable event. The photograph shows Oswald Cole in a position from which he would have had just a small chance of survival had the ice broken.

The article in the *Oxford Times* of February 1895 reads as follows:

THE GREAT FROST

The Great Frost, which will make the opening months of 1895 memorable and which has lasted with only a few days intermission since the 1st January at last shows signs of giving but its departure is not characterised by that celerity which most people would like to see. During the week there has been a considerable rise in the temperature and in the day time especially under the influence of the bright sun which has now gained considerable power the front surface of the ground has shown signs of a thaw and the unwonted sound of the trickle of water has been heard. The nights however have invariably been frosty with temperatures from 5-20 degrees being registered. The inconvenience to householders owing to the freezing of water pipes has been considerably increased during the week and there are very few houses where the supply has been maintained. Another result of the frost is the interruption of the sanitary arrangements and a rumour was current in the University at the end of last week that in the event of a continuance of the frost the authorities contemplated sending the men down thus prematurely bringing the term to a close. The rumour however lacks confirmation and with the change in the weather it is to be hoped that this unusual course which would disastrously affect the trade of the City may not have to be adopted. The water works officials are supplying water to householders from standpipes in the streets and by means of water carts which call from door to door. The partial thaw has had the effect of rendering the ice on the rivers unsafe but skating has been continued on the frozen floods and other places including Blenheim Lake where there is no stream and ice carnivals have been the order of the day.

*   ***Local distress****. We are in receipt of letters on going to press from the Rev. George Moore (Cowley), C. Broadhurst and J.H. Russell (New Hinksey), 'a worker' (St. Clements) and others for which we have no space referring to the great distress prevalent in Oxford and district owing to the long and severe frost and the general stoppage of out door work thus occasioned. We are informed of several acts of personal generosity and private benevolence and the Labourers' Association tender their thanks for valued assistance to the Reverend J. Carter, Messrs. T. Dodd, F.O. Stocker, Higgins, Kingerlee, Turrill, Cooper and Taphouse. Relief in kind will be given at Pusey House lecture rooms next Tuesday.*

*   *Five soup kitchens are now in full operation in the City and all of them have been well patronised from day to day. Over £100*

has been spent in distributing coal to needy persons by the Mayor. 3725 farthing breakfasts have been given at the Salvation Army Barracks during the severe weather. The food is supplied by the Mayor. They will be continued during the bad weather.

Coaching on the Isis. *With a continuance of the present arctic weather coaching on the Isis will lose the novelty which attached to it when Mr. James Porter of St. Aldates Street about four years ago drove his coach and four down mid-stream between the barges and the Long Bridges this feat having been three times performed within the last few days. This year the limits within which Mr. Porter has been enabled to manoeuvre his team have been somewhat circumscribed owing to the channels made through the ice for allowing punts to cross the stream. However a stretch of about fifty yards in length below Queens Barge has been available and the well-known 'whip' has been giving his friends the pleasure and gratification of a coach ride on the bosom of Father Thames. The first occasion was on Friday last when Mr. Porter drove onto the ice from the Grandpoint side of the river with a coach drawn by four horses and containing eight passengers. The teams had been especially shod with steel spiked shoes which admirably suited the purpose. The ice was composed of large flows frozen together and the travelling naturally was very rough but the weight of the turnout had no appreciable effect. On Saturday morning Mr. Porter repeated the novel experiment with a team of six horses. At the same time his daughter Miss N. Porter tooled a phaeton and his son rode on horseback on the ice, the party being afterwards photographed. On Monday the usual drive assumed importance owing to the presence of the Mayor who mounted the box seat after various evolutions had been performed by Mr. Porter in order to demonstrate to His Worship the safety of the venture. Among those who accompanied the Chief Magistrate of the City apparently with a view to contingencies were Superintendent Head and Inspector Cole while one of the inside passengers was an ex Councillor well known for his enormous weight about which he seemed to have uneasy* misgivings for he appeared at the door with an anxious expression on his features each time the coach stopped and finally quitted it with an undisguised air of relief. This was the fifth time Mr. Porter has performed a similar journey. Before 1891 it was forty years since such a feat was practicable.

Sheep roasting on the ice. On Monday a sheep was roasted on the Isis opposite Christ Church Barge. A fireplace was constructed of an iron hurdle supported on bricks the carcass being placed on a spit in front of the fire. The unusual scene attracted a large crowd among whom the meat was distributed when partially cooked.

2. Oswald to the left of the driver

I would like to say a special thank you to the *Oxford Mail* and *Oxford Times* and to their Managing Director, Shamus Donald, for giving me permission to use so much material from their pages. Without their help my task would have been impossible.

The *Oxford Mail* and *Oxford Times* have been using 'Cole' quotes for over one hundred years, as well as keeping a wonderful record of Oxford's social history during that period.

THE COLE FAMILY: OSWALD COLE

OSWALD COLE (MY GRANDFATHER) was born in Cheetham in Manchester in 1861 and moved to Oxford in 1891 with his wife, Emma (née Buxton). He was an Inspector in the Oxford City Police. He was made the first Chief Constable of the City in 1897. They had eight children who survived childhood and two who did not. Oswald was forty-eight when the last child, Phyllis, was conceived. He died on 5 March 1924 and Emma (born on 24 October 1863) died on 6 December 1936.

Oswald was very keen on sport – especially the tug of war - and he was captain of the Oxford City Police Team. In fact, he was an official referee at the London Olympics in 1908 and my sister, Rosemary, has kept the medal awarded to him.

3. Referee Medal

4. Emma

5. Oswald

6. Oswald, Emma and their children
Back row, left to right: Maurice, Jack, Bernard, Bunny
Centre row, left to right: Dorothy, Emma, Oswald, Bessie
Front row, left to right: Margie, Phyllis

*7. Encaenia procession in The High, Oxford,
outside The Queen's College, 1897, led by Oswald*

*8. Oxford City Police Officers, 1903,
Oswald in the centre*

9. Crowds at Oswald's funeral procession

OSWALD JOHN BUXTON COLE (JACK)

THE ELDEST SON, Oswald John Buxton Cole (Jack), was born on 19 December 1890 in Wandsworth. Jack joined the police force and was later appointed Chief Constable of Worcester and finally Chief Constable of Leicester. He married Molly Hicks and they had one son (Edward John), known as Teddy, who served in the Second World War and for part of the time was with Bunny in Burma. Tragically, he was killed in a plane crash on his way home. Teddy's loss was particularly shattering to both Jack and Molly. With his position and general life experiences, Jack was able to bear his grief but Molly found it so very difficult.

10. Teddy in uniform

11. Jack in police uniform

When she herself was widowed on 26 September 1957 she was particularly distressed. I saw quite a lot of her over the years. She used to come and stay with us at Green Ridges, at Dunstan Road and with Sheila, my wife, and our family at Burford. She sought solace with a succession of dogs. They were, as far as I can remember, all called Coco and were usually poodles and, as their names would suggest, were named after their colour. They were not popular with my mother, Edith. They adopted the same modus operandi which was to arrive with great ceremony followed by charging into the house, up the stairs and returning to the ground floor with a succession of cockings of the leg against the best furniture. Edith would rush around afterwards with the appropriate cleaning material, assuring Molly that there was no harm done but secretly seething with rage. She made it very clear to Bunny that this was 'the last time', but when that time came she always relented.

Molly was small in stature and was not the most beautiful of women, which I remember rather rudely mentioning to one of her sisters-in-law. I was not only (and quite rightly) told off but it was explained to me that Molly in her teens or early twenties had been a fearless hockey goalkeeper, whose defensive actions on the pitch were the cause of the permanent damage to her face. As a hockey player myself her bravery put her high up the ladder in my estimation.

Her main claim to fame was playing bridge. I understand that Molly was indeed a good player and she would come to breakfast and relive some of the entire hands played the evening before, with Molly ending by making a grand slam. As children we were brought up to believe that she did play, or may have played, for England. Amongst her effects which were passed to me when she died were countless photographs of bridge achievements, accompanied by score cards etc.

When Molly came to stay the first thing that had to be organised was a game of bridge. This was not particularly difficult to arrange and Molly had numerous friends in the Oxford area who used to be delighted to play. However, as time passed they were less anxious to turn out and finally it was only the family who could be relied upon to make up the numbers. On one such occasion after her arrival she announced that we would play bridge. Bunny said that he had tried to find a fourth without success. At this Molly told him that there was no problem, indicating that I would partner Molly. Bunny remonstrated that I did not play but his objection was overruled and he was assured that she would look after me and we started to play. I was about thirteen at the time and at that time had never played bridge. We were not very far into the game when my inexperience came to the fore. I forget what I did but I suspect I trumped Molly's ace. The game ended in chaos to the shouts of, 'You stupid boy'. So far as I remember I tried to justify my position but by then my mother was in tears and I did not play again for about fifty years, by which time Molly had died. I am told that I do have a maverick style of bidding which may be the result of receiving unfair criticism at the bridge table – perhaps I should have had counselling.

Jack retired in 1955 and was succeeded by Robert Mark who later became the Commissioner of the Metropolitan Police. On 14 December 1955 a ceremony took place at the police headquarters in Leicester which was recorded in the *Police Chronicle* and *Constabulary World*; various tributes were paid and a winged easy chair was presented to Jack by Mr Ecob (the Deputy Chief Constable) on behalf of all ranks of the Force and its civilian staff. According to the press report this was followed by a 'surprise' presentation made by Inspector J Edwards and kept secret from Jack until the moment of presentation. The gift was a unique oak casket holding an illuminated address in the form of a scroll. The scroll designed and executed by Sergeant Edward Walker contained the following address:

To Oswald John Buxton Cole,
Commander of the Order of the British Empire,
1929 - Chief Constable – 1955

May it please you to accept this tribute – of our most loyal and sincere admiration of the manner in which you have commanded us throughout your appointment. Most especially do we wish to record our grateful thanks for the open-minded attitude you have displayed to each and every one of us and for your example to us all. It has been an honour and pleasure to serve you, Sir.

We wish you a happy retirement.

This scroll was signed by 340 members of the Force and civilian staff. The casket, which had been designed and made by

Police Constable Cecil Knight, was in oak and lined with blue velvet. With the casket is the following inscription:

The wood from which this casket is made has been selected for its association with your appointment here as Chief Constable, as follows:-

Front and rear skirting - from a worn floor board removed from Welford Police Box.

Front Panel - from the broken door of the Charge Office waiting room, smashed by a prisoner.

Legs - from an oak stake used for denoting unexploded bombs.

Top - from a table, damaged by air attack and salvaged from the Knighton tip.

Ends - from the wood used as packing-cases when your personal belongings were sent back after your recruiting mission abroad.

12. Casket and scroll

In making the presentation Inspector Edwards said, 'Maybe, Sir, this parchment has little monetary value but it's true value is shown by the fact that it is signed by nearly everyone connected with the force. Therein lies it's intrinsic worth – the tribute – to you, Sir, which I presume to say far outshines anything you have received or may receive, however expensive it may be, because it clearly indicates the goodwill existing towards you and the high regard in which you are held by all ranks of the force.'

Of course, Jack did not start life as Chief Constable. He moved with his parents to Oxford and at the outbreak of war in 1914 he enlisted and was commissioned into the Royal Artillery. Unfortunately, he was captured at Cambrai only a few weeks after joining his battery and spent the rest of the war in German prison camps at Karlsberg and Heidelberg.

13. Photo of prison camp, Jack in centre

Jack was quite clearly the head of the family after Oswald died although Emma, as far as one can infer from various notes and letters, took a very active part in controlling and keeping in touch with the family. An example is to be found as to what happened after George Langley (Margie's husband) died in 1943. Margie, who was one of Oswald's daughters, was going to be left short of funds and it was Jack who organised the family finances so that all the wage earners could make a contribution each week. George had been manager of a branch of the Westminster Bank and his last posting was at Babbacombe, near Torquay. Margie's three children, Celia, Christopher (Kiff) and Caroline, were settled in Devon and it seemed that although all were anxious to help, the need for a formal arrangement did not become necessary. I suspect that the bank was more generous than had been expected. Be that as it may, the family did help in so many ways, not only Margie but others as well.

Jack was a great character and his visits with Molly were splendid occasions and their visits immediately became a great excuse to throw parties. Sometimes merriment got out of control and on one occasion Jack decided that he was throwing out some of his shirts or perhaps the last wash had been too severe and there had been violent shrinkage. On this visit Jack brought with him a pile of shirts which were eagerly pounced upon by Bunny and Maurice. Such was their alacrity that Jack thought he would try one on himself in case they need not be passed on at that time. Jack had an impressive chest and stripped off his shirt to try on one of the other shirts. It looked fine but then he started to expand his chest and as he did so one of the buttons had had enough and flew off at speed. Unfortunately, it struck my mother (Edith) on the arm and we all hooted with laughter, although it must have been extremely painful. Jack was quick to apologise and chastised himself for being so stupid. He warned us all that such conduct could have caused serious injury. We all agreed and the laughter started again but we had learned an important lesson.

Whether it was on the same visit I do not remember but Edith had saved what would have been a large amount of money which she could not afford to buy a giant bottle of Eau de Cologne lotion which she had presented to Bunny. He was delighted with it and put the bottle on the sideboard in the dining room. It was spotted by Jack who remarked upon its size and as to how similar in shape it was to a rugby ball. Enough said, because either Jack or Bernard picked it up and passed it to the other. It was caught and returned but inevitably the passes got more difficult until it was dropped and the bottle exploded. If only they had remembered the family phrase 'a joke twice repeated loses its charm' etc. all would have been well. We all felt an element of guilt but whatever degree had to be attached to us either as principals or aiders and abetters we all suffered. The liquid fell on the magnificently laden fruit bowl. We tried to wash the fruit but however much we tried we could not avoid the smell or taste of the cologne in the dining room for a long time to come.

Jack had a wonderful sense of humour, which was evident in the contents of a family album which seems to have been started by Molly in 1906 and contributed to by Jack and Bessie in 1909. 'He that sitteth on a needle's point shall rise quickly' (OJBC 1909 Mar 9). Later in the book was a small poem which deserves mention:

A Moving Tale

There was a dachshund once so long,
You haven't any notion
The time it took to notify
His tail of his emotion.
And thus it happened, while his eyes
Would weep with woe and sadness
His tail would still be waggin' on
Because of previous gladness.

M. Jones Nov 21 1906

14. Jack, Mollie, Dorothy, Bebe and Elizabeth

SHADES OF BEDFORD HOUSE

15. 'I want to introduce my son.'
'What on earth for?'

Dear Bernard

Have you ever seen a better portrayal of Tommy Robinson and at 'A'. Could you guess at 'B' and 'C'? Please note and pass on to Maurice to ………

(signed) *Jack 12.1.37*

A perfect example of Realism. It is now clear that our Brother Raymie was once an artist's model but the years have treated him unkindly – he hasn't changed a bit!

(signed) *Bernard*

It might have been me!

(signed) *Maurice*

Marvellous likenesses of B & co. How well I remember Bunny like that – the phrase I remember best is 'Pax, Maurice, while I take my specs off!'

(signed) *Dorothy*

To Bunny's chin:-
'So was it when my life began,
 So is it now I am a man,
 So be it when I shall grow old,
Or let me die!'

Wordsworth

(signed) *B   25.1.37*

Remembrance of 'A' and 'B' fair, 'C' screamingly funny!
(signed) *Margaret 29-1-37*

The only time I remember having seen Tommy Robinson – usually referred to by a most unpleasant nickname – was during an air raid when Raymond was dragged from under the table and stood in the exact position and with the exact expression on his face which is portrayed in this picture, but he was wearing one of Bessie's dressing gowns – a pale mauve one with a grey fur collar!
(signed) *Phyllis   7.2.37*

Wherever we lived as a family I remember this cartoon either hanging on the wall or propped up on a mantelpiece and when Bunny and Edith died it was passed to me. I used to look at it most days and would have a chuckle but it was not until I finally took possession of it that I realised there was writing on the back.

EARLY NOTES NARRATED BY BUNNY (PART I)

I SUPPOSE THAT everyone has tried to remember his earliest recollection of all. I have three very early recollections but cannot say which came first. I remember sitting between my parents in their double bed and being conscious that I was safe. Safe from bogeymen and shadows and giants – absolutely safe!

I remember, it must have been a little later on, creeping along the corridor at Ebor House where we lived to listen at the door of my parents to make sure that they had not died during the night. It was a great relief to hear my father snoring so that I could go back contentedly to bed.

The other recollection is of being taken to watch the Oxford City Police play cricket against one of the colleges on a huge cricket field in Cowley Road. My father had a beautiful Sunbeam bicycle with a little oil bath which the chain ran through. A red cushion was tied onto the crossbar for me to sit on with my feet hardly touching the top of the forks. We got there safely, having overtaken one of the horse trams en route, and I watched my first cricket match with my mother who must have got there by some other means.

One of our side, Ted Massey, who was said to be the best batsman in the Force, was scoring runs well and confidently although I did not realise his prowess at the time. What I do remember is that a fast ball came off his bat and hit him in his private parts and when I asked my mother what was the matter with him she said, 'Poor man' as she looked the other way. 'He has been struck in a very tender place. I do hope that he will be all right. I must go and speak to Mrs Massey.'

Another fairly early recollection of mine which gave me intense pride in my father and his Force was the Oxford City

Police sports held at the Oxford University running ground when our team defeated the City of London Police in the final of the tug-of-war; an enormous silver cup was the trophy. After due celebrations in the pavilion, in which I was not allowed to take part because of my age, we journeyed from the ground in a hansom cab to Ebor House, Blue Boar Street, Oxford, where we lived. I was privileged to stand up and hold the cup for everyone to see as we drove triumphantly over Magdalen Bridge and along The High and clattered to a halt outside our house. I was proud of my father who was the captain. I was proud of the team and of the police of Oxford.

It is a wonderful experience anyway to travel in a hansom cab. The driver is perched up above you and if you want to speak to him you shout round the side of the cab or tap on the roof and the cabby opens a little window in the roof and talks to you from his upside-down position above. The horse clatters along, usually making rude noises and smells which the passengers pretend not to notice. Edith tells a lovely story on this subject: Mrs Enid Lane Fox MBE told her of the occasion when she was being driven by a groom who had collected her from the railway station to take her to Blenheim Palace for a meeting and the horse broke wind. The groom apologised profusely and Mrs Lane Fox said, 'Do not worry, Simkins, I thought it was the horse.'

My father, Dad, the *pater*, Ossie, the old man - according to who and what you were - always thought of and called himself a Yorkshire man despite being born in Manchester, but in his early life he lived at Bishopsthorpe, just outside York. He married my mother, Emma Anne Buxton, and they had ten children, eight of whom reached adulthood. One (Sydney) died as a child and another (Kitty) died as a very young baby. My mother was born in Norwich and later went to Barnard Castle in Durham. She often told us that when she and her brothers and sisters arrived in Durham they were mimicked because of their sing-song speech and were asked to give demonstrations. I think her father may have been a railwayman. Whatever he was his children were all well spoken, well educated and well mannered. My mother was very shy but could talk with anyone and became a bright light in the Christian Science Movement, becoming one of the two readers.

Mother worked in a furrier's shop in York and was adept at working with fur and this was evident all through her life. If ever anyone had a fur coat or anything made of fur which was the worse for wear Mother would repair it most skilfully. It was incredible how fur garments lasted in the family for years and years, getting smaller and smaller as time went by. I remember one particular white coat which I think went right through the family and finished with Phyllis. It may even eventually have been turned into a white evening cape for Phyllis, known by her doting oldest sister, Bess, as 'toy child'.

The same happened with carpets, which I remember were sometimes in a dreadful state until one day there was a protest meeting held by the children, demanding a new carpet for the dining room. Dad and Mother thought we might get one through Uncle Gilbert (Longland) who was the husband of Dad's sister, Edith, who had a big furniture shop in Birmingham. Dad went to Birmingham, probably by bicycle, and came back to say that he had bought the carpet. He did not know how much and had not chosen one. He had told Uncle Gilbert that we would like one with red and white in it. It arrived a week later, a red and white striped carpet. It lasted for years and we got used to it.

Post script: It was not until Sheila and I moved to Warwickshire that we had any contact with that branch of the family and we did so through a cousin, Poppy, who was living with her family in Canada. We met Peter Longland and his wife, Sheila. Peter was the Chairman of Lee Longlands. We found them to be friendly and delightful company and met up with them on many occasions, including a visit to our house when we were entertaining

Andrew and Jandy Tipping who were on holiday from New Zealand.

I am told that I was a very crotchety baby. I think I had convulsions or some such and when this occurred I would have to be suddenly immersed in a hot bath. Despite this I grew up fit and with reasonably good lungs. John, my youngest son, who must still hold the record for crying at his christening, has good lungs and so, too, I hope will David, his son, having nearly equalled his father's record in the same church at Wolvercote many years later.

My first school was a baby school in Wellington Square, Oxford, which was run by some nuns who lived in a convent between St Giles and Wellington Square. I remember my first day at school when I was a dreadful nuisance to everybody at first, but I gradually got used to it and in the end quite enjoyed it. I was allowed to take Margaret (Margie) my sister to school, which I found very flattering, and she quite enjoyed it too. One day on our way to school we became involved in an incident with a hansom cab. I did not notice it coming and we were in the process of crossing the road when it suddenly bore down upon us. In the event the wheel went over my knee but Margaret was not touched as far as I know. I got a certain amount of undue credit for bravery in the *Oxford Journal Illustrated* which gave an exaggerated account in my favour of what had happened. The *Oxford Journal* used to be published every Wednesday.

My next school was the Boys' Central School in Gloucester Green which I enjoyed very much. I was there from about the age of six until I was ten years old, when I was transferred to Bedford House School, of which Tommy Robinson was headmaster and a great personal friend of my father. I enjoyed my time at Bedford House, except that I was always rather afraid of Tommy Robinson who could be delightful and charming but to a young boy he was a fearsome spectacle when angered, as he frequently was. He said on one occasion, 'Why should I spend my time trying to teach you? I am a Master of Arts of this celebrated university – it is intolerable.' Those sort of tirades were quite common and by the time one had grown to the age of fourteen or so one did not take so very much notice of them. So my last two years at school were enjoyable and I developed a desire to learn, certainly during my last year at school. I also became head of the school in that I was captain of football and sat in one of the two best places in the class. Bedford House Old Boys' Club was formed and I went to the first dinner, arranged for about a dozen of us, and at which event Tommy Robinson was invited to dine with us. So the club was formed and the dinner was held pretty regularly from then on even though the school had been closed.

During the First World War we had many scares and excitements. The first wounded coming into Oxford were met and fêted and generous subscriptions were raised to provide them with goodies.

When Belgium was invaded there was a Belgian flag day and it was socially important to have a table and sell the flags in the colours of red, black and yellow of 'our gallant little allies.'

My family stall was run by my mother with Dorothy (my sister) and various social ladies and was well placed outside The Mitre Hotel, where Miss Thorn was the manageress. She was a friend of my father and mother. I had several teas and ices on that occasion which, at the age of ten years, was my first experience of eating for charity.

The country went wild with excitement and delight at the end of a ghastly period in the history of the country. I later understood that we lost 'the flower of our manhood.' I was disappointed. I had hoped that the war would not end until I had been able to go into the army so that I could serve my country, as had my brothers and sister, and a card could be put in the window to go with those for Jack, Bess and Bernard.

I saw the First World War through the eyes of a boy from the ages of ten to fourteen, and was fourteen and a half when the armistice was signed at 11 a.m. on 11 November 1918. The news was given to us in Bedford House School, Oxford, by the headmaster, Tommy Robinson. He subdued the spontaneous cheering by saying that he had some further news. He said, 'My eldest son died this morning in Somerville College from the flu.' We had known that the man was ill in hospital in Oxford but had not known of the tragic course of the dreadful epidemic. Harry was a Lieutenant in the Oxfordshire and Buckinghamshire Light Infantry.

When I was about eleven years of age there was a time when the frequent topic of adult conversation at Ebor House was about a comet which was going to fly over Oxford. We were told that it was like a star with a fiery tail. Its exact date and time of arrival had been calculated, or so it was said by my father and three wise brothers and four sisters. So at the right time Dad took me into the Oxford University Parks to see it. I cannot remember how long we had to wait but it seemed only a few minutes after our arrival that we saw it. We were in the southeast corner of the parks, towards the pathway to Parson's Pleasure and to Mesopotamia. It was high in the sky. It was travelling in a south-easterly direction and travelling over Joe Pullen's tree and on over Cowley. It was just like a big yellow star with a wiggly tail. In a few minutes it had gone out of sight. I have checked the date of its passage over England and it apparently occurred in 1915.

DEUM COLE REGEM SERVA

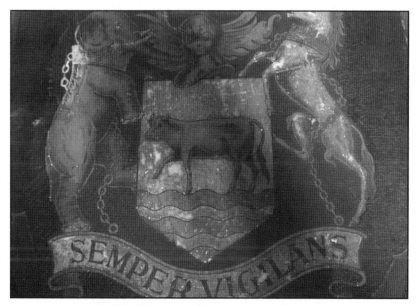

*16. Shield removed from the black maria
used by the Oxford City Police*

I LIKE OUR FAMILY MOTTO which, if I am accurate in my translation of it, means 'Honour God and serve the king.' Honour seems to me to be the correct word to describe one's duty to God and to serve the king is also exactly right.

My father, Oswald, was Chief Constable of the City of Oxford and had been since 1897. He died in harness in 1924. He was a royalist, a loyalist and a nationalist. He put duty before everything else and his sense of duty was very strongly defined. He believed sleep to be a blessed thing and hated people to be awakened except when they had to go on duty. That included going to work and when you were not fit and too young going to school. He joined and served in the Metropolitan Police in V and A Divisions and moved to Oxford as an Inspector in the Oxford City Force under the Superintendent Head on 30 July 1891. The Superintendent retired on a pension on 12 March 1897 and Oswald was appointed Chief Constable. He was the first ever Chief Constable of the City of Oxford and served as such for just under twenty-seven years. He was, in my recollection, very often called the Super instead of Chief, though gradually over the years we were glad that he got to be called 'Chief'. He was extraordinarily well known and respected. He had one or two difficult patches in his police life and although I was too young to know much about them at the time I knew more about them later. I think that he was more than once criticised for dealing with culprits himself. He would send for recalcitrant cab drivers and lawbreaking landlords and tell them off in his office instead of prosecuting, and I do not think he was ever let down by those to whom he administered his summary jurisdiction. There were, of course, always similar cases where prosecutions took place and it was felt by many, no doubt rightly, that the Magistrates and not the Chief should adjudicate. My own belief is that each one of us must have the right if he has the power to decide when to save someone from the purgatory of press publicity. Oswald had a Shakespearean quotation, which I have not authenticated, which I suspect he coined himself: 'As ye are strong be ye also merciful.'

He loved the soldiers and was intensely proud when, at the age of sixteen my brother, Bernard, came down from Liverpool to Oxford to join up in the Oxfordshire Yeomanry Q00H to go to war – the Kaiser's War. Bernard went to sign on at Christ Church, Oxford with Jack Wilsdon, who was two years older than him. Jack, who looked about sixteen, was told he could not be accepted but Bernard got through because they believed him when he said he was eighteen. Jack Wilsdon got in a few hours later, having gone home to get his birth certificate. I remember going down St Aldates to see Bernard on guard at the meadow entrance to 'Christ

Church' which was then Yeomanry headquarters. The entrance was then by a cobbled roadway flanked to the south side by the stables. It was one of the saddle rooms which had been converted into the Guard Room. There, Bernard was on guard with carbine and shiny silver buttons. I think Q00H was the only regiment in the British army with silver buttons.

As a young boy I was always running errands for everybody and anybody and I did very well in a small way with 'thank you' tips. I remember earning six pence for taking a pair of puttees and a uniform jacket from the OTC stores under the Town Hall in our yard to St John's College. Bess (my sister Mary Elizabeth) did not like that at all. I often did the shopping and paid some of the small bills for my mother and I remember two particular disasters:

On one occasion I dropped a golden half sovereign down the drain in High Street at the top of our yard. I remember thinking of the awful consequences if I did drop it and I was careful to hold it tightly until I had passed the drain and then, for some extraordinary reason, I released my grip and the half sovereign dropped onto the ground and rolled along and between the bars of the drain. An old lady saw it happen and marshalled help and the half sovereign was recovered in response to my fervent prayers.

The other tragedy was when Dorothy (my sister) had given me a bottle of strawberry syrup to flavour the ice cream we were making that Sunday morning and having held it for greater care under my coat dropped it in Bear Lane and lost its delicious contents. Looking back it does not seem to have mattered too much because the Sunday ice cream we made once or twice each summer only tasted of the salt we put in the ice to stop it melting.

My father was of a big family and all his brothers and sisters had only one Christian name – with the exception of the eldest, Edwin John. The boys had either Saxon or Norman names. The order was Edwin, Oswald, Edgar, Alfred, Harold, Lambert and Gilbert. There were three sisters – Mildred, Edith and Winifred. I do not know what Edwin did. Harold had a bicycle shop in Rugby but unfortunately he did not emulate Lord Nuffield. Lambert had a good job as a Land Agent for one of the Watkin-Wynnes and lived for some time in Stowmarket and later near Ruabon. He was a captain in the First World War with the Welsh Fusiliers and was a very smart soldier with his black flash and military bearing. All the Coles of that generation, and I think perhaps of this generation, looked good in uniform.

I used to love to see my father heading a procession dressed in his Chief Constable's uniform and with his medals. It was often said of him that he was a fine figure of a man and there is no doubt that, in my eyes at least, he gave a dignity to the ceremonial occasions in which he took part.

My mother's older sister, Mary, was a Roman Catholic, having married a young man named Maycock who died very young, and she became Matron of Blundells, the Roman Catholic public school. Her son, Martin, did very well in the railways and became one of the chief engineers of the old London and North Eastern Railway. Her younger sister, Aunt Louisa, was a dear and a great favourite in the family.

As soon as my brothers and sisters got old enough they all departed from the nest but came home whenever they could.

The eldest child of Oswald and Emma was Jack and he was educated at New College School, Oxford (Maurice was there too) and then to the University Observatory in the Parks for about a year and then went to Brighton as a boy in the police office under Sir William Gentle, the Chief Constable, who was a personal friend of my father. He stayed until he went to the war.

Bernard was sent to Liverpool where he was in the police office and he stayed there until he returned to Oxford to go to war.

Bess (Mary Elizabeth) was educated at Milham Ford School in Oxford and then went to a teacher training college at Camberwell, which she hated. She later became a teacher at Stoke Lyne School in Oxfordshire where she met and married her husband, Edward Hillsdon, who was the son of the local blacksmith.

Dorothy, my eldest sister, got married in 1911 to Andrew Walsh who was a very well-known and successful solicitor in Oxford. At one time Andrew was in partnership with Frank Gray, one of Oxford's characters, just before and after the war. I was articled to Cecil Bartram, one of the partners, in 1923 and I was admitted as a Solicitor of the Supreme Court in 1928. Andrew had a great influence on the Cole family. He brought a bubbling fearless sense of humour with him. He would make a joke out of anything, even the most serious of matters, and loved to pull people's legs. At a very early age I remember roaring with laughter when he asked my mother with a serious face if the china cupboard door could be closed because there was such a draught. I used to chaperone Dorothy sometimes and remember sumptuous teas which included, I remember, a whole honeycomb and all kinds of scones and cakes. Supreme of all was a cream and toffee cake from Buols, a wonderful cake shop in Cornmarket, situated just about where WH Smiths is now. It was later to become Dijon and then Stewart's before eventually disappearing with the Tunnel, the pub next door, between the wars. The toffee cake consisted of alternate layers of caramel cream and toffee. It needed a sharp pointed knife to cut it without squelching all its delicious ingredients over the cake plate. It was an absolute joy to eat. I think Dorothy and Andrew were very much in love and I remember obtaining their approbation for my hummed rendering of what I believe was the waltz from the Merry Widow.

As a family we did not have ordinary holidays. I do not think I ever went to the seaside before I was about twelve, except for one visit to Southsea which I do not remember. However, I do remember a photograph which was taken of me in a little goat cart with my brother Maurice. Our holidays were nearly always spent camping and we enjoyed them immensely.

The earliest camp I remember was at Pinkhill; a subsequent one at Eynsham and then one or more at Godstow and later back

17. Goat cart and the pram

to Eynsham, before coming back to Godstow where we used to camp in what is now the car park of The Trout Public House. I have all sorts of memories of the Godstow camp especially because that is where I first swam the river at a very young age under the command of Basher Webb who was then a Sergeant in the Oxford City Police Force, having previously served in the Royal Marines and later becoming Deputy Chief Constable of Oxford. He was a very powerful swimmer and had a huge stentorian voice. He took me over to the other side of the river and then swam off himself and told me to follow him. He swam quickly to the other side, turned around and shouted to me to come on. In the end I managed to develop the necessary courage and started - only to pause right in the middle of the deepest part of the river as the water started to bubble around me. His roar frightened me. He galvanised me into action and I swam out for the shore which I duly gained. From then on I was never afraid to swim anywhere and not even afraid to go in the punt 'down danger' which was what frightened Margaret, my sister, most of all. There was a big 'danger' sign warning people not to get into the stream which ran sometimes at a very fast rate down to the lasher at The Trout.

At all our camps we seemed to be invaded by plagues of wasps. We used to have jam pot traps with a little jam or beer in the bottom and then some water and the wasps would go into the pot and were usually too drunk or jammed up to be able to get out. The practice was to empty the jam pot every day or more often behind a willow tree on the bank of the river. Unfortunately, if it became necessary to venture behind the said tree for some reason or another and one stepped in the heap of corpses of wasps one could get quite badly stung. Presumably, the wasps' stings are still operative after death or some of them might still have been alive.

One of the best short holidays on the river I ever had was when my father and I cycled to Surbiton where Uncle Gilbert (Cole) lived. His wife was away and we stayed the night in his flat and had a very good evening meal. I gained immediate favour by removing a large spider for Uncle Gilbert. He had a spider phobia.

The next day we started to row or rather scull from Surbiton to Oxford in a double sculler. It was very leisurely and very comfortable. We had picnic lunches but we had breakfast and dinner in hotels en route.

I cannot remember which hotels we stayed at except that I well remember staying at The Angel at Henley-on-Thames because I had to sleep in the same bed with Uncle Gilbert who snored all night, and I do not think that I got a single wink of sleep.

It may as well be said now that the Cole family likes its drink. Uncle Gilbert and my father were no exception on this three men in a boat trip. Uncle Gilbert, as the host, had seen to it that there was plenty of whisky and soda aboard. After about 11.00 a.m. it was usually time for one of them to ask me if I would like a bottle of ginger beer or some lime juice and when I accepted, as I always did, Uncle Gilbert would say, 'We had better keep the boy company, Oswald' and he always agreed. The whisky was taken out and a nice leisurely interlude was enjoyed by all of us. Uncle Gilbert was a keen photographer and when we were looking through the photographs on some later occasion I earned quite a reputation as a wit by pointing out the inevitable glass on the table in the picture. I can't work out what year this would have been but I suspect it must have been 1915 or thereabouts. I believe I was about twelve at the time.

At various times of my life I have travelled the whole of the Thames by boat of one kind or another. We usually hired a double or treble sculler from David Talboys near Folly Bridge and usually went upstream. Later, we would hire a cabin cruiser from Salters so that it must have been in 1919 that my three brothers and myself and Aubrey King as an extra went up to Lechlade in a triple sculler, having arranged a very clever method of getting a rest and changing positions. We drew lots to start with to see who should be cox/stroke/two power house/bow and rest man. Then at each lock we would move up one so that the rest man would become cox etc.

There was a lot of luck in this because some locks were only about a mile apart and others as much as three or four miles apart and it was not long before some of the older and cleverer or perhaps less scrupulous members of the party, with the aid of a map of the Thames, worked out the distances and when it would be their turn. Then, by judicious offerings of half a bar of chocolate or such like they managed to get their positions changed.

There was a certain amount of horseplay and on one occasion Maurice was stroke and complained that No. 2 and bow were not keeping proper time with him. In the laughter which ensued Maurice got bumped in the back and said that the other oarsmen might as well not row as he was pulling along the whole boat himself anyway. At that the others stopped rowing because we happened to have just got to a narrow part of the river with a consequently faster flowing stream which took the boat backwards rather more quickly than Maurice could pull it forward.

A camping trick which I learned at a very early age was how not to fill a palliasse (which is a mattress filled with straw) too tightly, to refill it the next day after it has worn down but never fill it tight for its first use and never pretend to understand a primus stove if you don't. The whole secret of using a primus is when to start pumping. On one occasion when we were going down stream in the 1920s in a cabin cruiser someone in the crew, who shall remain nameless, having assured me that he understood the primus stove proceeded to light it as we went through Sandford Lock. He started to pump too soon, lost his nerve when he saw the liquid paraffin ignite and tried to hold the stove under the water to put out the flame. The flames, of course, lapped round his hand and wrist and he had to drop the primus in the river at one of its deepest parts just in the downstream pool outside the lock gates. On this same trip we had great fun towing people at the end of a rope from the back of the cabin cruiser. We were going along by that lovely stretch of Harts Lock Woods just above Pangbourne when I nearly drowned Aubrey King. He was holding onto the rope and I accelerated to the maximum speed of the craft and to my horror I realised that he was totally submersed.

I learnt quite a lot in my camping holidays. I learnt the sort of things that one does pick up from experience and can only learn by oneself. The sort of thing I have in mind is that if you only have one pillow and you are sleeping rough you should consider using it for your hip instead of for your head.

If you are sleeping on sand or in some other malleable resting place it should be easy enough to hollow out a basin for one of your hips to rest in.

Another thing to remember is that to sleep warm you must keep your head warm and it is much better to wrap your sweater around your head rather than to wear it if you are limited in bed clothes. A vital thing to remember is that you must have as much under you as over you if you are to sleep warm. Finally, if you are sleeping in a boat or, indeed, if you are in charge of a boat never moor it with a short painter because if the river rises or falls you are likely to end up with your boat submerged half under water. I had an experience of that at Godstow when we were camping and a sudden drop in the river level caused the boat to assume quite a dangerous angle because it was moored too tightly.

Years later in Burma I had a similar experience when in command of a flotilla of motor boats. I had to navigate some tidal chaungs in the dark to get to a rendezvous before dawn to evacuate casualties from an attack which the 11th Sikhs were putting in near Maungdaw. We arrived at our rendezvous about an hour before dawn and moored our boats and after posting guards in strategic positions, so far as the enemy was concerned we had left the boats to look after themselves.

We were very lucky. The tide was on the ebb and in a very short time the level of water had dropped by three or four feet so that our boats were at a dangerous angle which was noticed just in time to save them. I had not learned by my experience at The Trout thirty years before but I shall remember next time.

Other incidents at Godstow camp were numerous. I am reputed to have swallowed Bernard's minnows which he had been keeping for bait but I cannot remember that. What I do, however, remember is being put on the operating table to have a fishhook removed from my ankle by Bernard after he had sterilised a dirty old penknife by holding it in the flame of a candle.

Christ Church Meadow was a wonderful place and I have always been an opponent of any road project to run through it.

My very early days were spent largely in the meadow where we found birds' nests and snakes and all manner of wild flowers and much joy in trotting right round the meadow behind Dad on his constitutional or lolling in the sun in Dead Man's Walk and going to the botanical gardens on the fringe of the meadow. Here we had special treatment because my father knew Mr Baker, who was the resident Headman. I even remember being given a Canary banana which had grown in one of the hothouses.

We went to see the fish very frequently and my father knew the trick of attracting them, which was to tap his keys on the rose of the miniature fountain. At once the water was red and gold with fish who scrambled for their crumbs.

When he was about ten I took James, my eldest grandson, to see the fish carrying out the same routine. However, an attendant said, 'You must not feed the fish. They are not allowed to eat bread as it is bad for them.' One had to accept his orders and I am sure he was right but I was tempted to say that I had done the same thing fifty or so years before and no apparent harm to the fish had resulted, nor had they suffered from impaired growth.

Dorothy had five charming beautiful daughters and no sons. I have been blessed with beautiful nieces by blood and marriage. I remember especially the delight of shopping with Dorothy through the market on Saturday mornings and finishing up at the Cadena where the most delicious ice cream was made in all kinds of varieties. I chose the exotic ones sometimes but rarely could I resist my favourite strawberry ice.

Aubrey King used to come with us frequently. He was my best friend and Frank, his elder brother was Maurice's friend. We used to go for walks together in Christ Church Meadow whenever we could and that was really the place where we played and got our exercise. Sometimes we went further afield to the Chilswell hills over the lake bridge and South Hinksey but rarely to the university parks which is odd because they always were very beautiful. The reason for our propensity to go south was because we had a little garden or allotment opposite the White House public house in Abingdon Road and we grew an immense amount of produce and had apple trees and flowers. It was a short stage past Christ Church Meadow and on the way to the Chilswell Hills. We did go to the university parks one day on a Sunday morning and I, in my new best Sunday suit, was playing with water beetles when I fell into the river and was hauled out by Bernard. I was covered with chickweed and I went home in great fear and trembling. Strangely enough, I was not rebuked and neither was Bernard, who never seemed to get blamed very much and most of his escapades went unpunished.

We had a little yard at the back of Ebor House in Blue Boar Street. During the First World War everyone was urged to keep rabbits and chickens so that we could live on them and we had a go at most things. We had a lot of rabbits from time to time but could never bring ourselves to kill them and they had to be taken away by the butcher and then we would not eat them if we knew that they were ours. The chickens were not so bad and one day my mother got Mr Bliss, the caretaker of the single men's quarters of the police station just behind our house, to ring the neck of a little bantam type cock who always woke everyone in the early hours of the morning. The little cock was duly dealt with and hung up by his feet on the clothes line. Passing along the passage which looked on to this little yard my mother saw the cock give a mournful but deliberate wink as she went by. She rushed out with a knife and cut the poor thing down. He staggered about with his head on one side and so he remained for the rest of his life but he never crowed again and eventually died a natural death.

The family was close-knit and backed each other up. If ever I was sent to bed without supper for misbehaving, which was very frequently, I could always rely on somebody, usually Margaret, smuggling some food up to me.

Before Margaret was old enough it was Sarah who was my ally. Sarah was our little old-fashioned maid-of-all-work. Her surname was Allen and she came from Steeple Aston. It was she who gave me, or perhaps only threatened to give me, the brush – a stiff bristled hairbrush – on the bottom. I think she did give it to me once but she threatened it many times and perhaps the sight of my tender naked behind may have encouraged preparation for the punishment but perhaps its soft rounded defencelessness made the kind-hearted soul unable to leave her mark upon it.

Dad must have gone through some very poignant times when he saw off Bernard, then Bess and later Jack to the war.

I remember the grey November Saturday morning when Dad brought me my cup of tea in bed with the news which he could hardly speak: 'Poor old Jack is missing.' So he was and we feared the worst and hoped for the blessed news which duly came about a fortnight later that he was a prisoner of war and safe and well.

Perhaps this waiting period was especially harrowing for Dad who had encouraged Jack to join up.

I was just a little ashamed of myself that after hearing the bad news I ate a good breakfast and went off to play football. That is how I know it was a Saturday morning.

My father had a wonderful sense of humour and put up with an immense amount of insubordination from eight children with twenty years between the oldest (Jack) and the youngest (Phyllis). The older children were I think better mannered in the parental presence than the youngest (except for Margaret who was nearly always well behaved and dutiful to her parents.)

My dear kind mother once struck Margaret a blow because she had hit me with a toy gun. I rounded on Mother for hitting her. Loyalties in a family are a funny thing and usually mean that you side with the one in trouble.

Whenever Bernard or Bess came home on leave from France the house was agog with excitement. They always contrived to bring some super French sweets with them. I remember Bess, when on leave from Rouen, brought some beautiful sticky sweets rather like rock but of solid sugar in beautiful colours and flavoured with cherry (cerise) and other luscious flavours. *(Author's note: I remember shortly after my father's return and demob him taking my mother on a weekend trip to Rouen and bringing back for me and Rose many different colours of the rock.)*

The nougat too was beautiful but it was not really the sweets I looked for from either of them. I looked for souvenirs: German bullets, cap badges, bomb splinters, pieces of barbed wire from Loos, chalk with battle names carved upon them and a whole unused field dressing and a button from a French soldier's coat. These were the things that really mattered, but the sweets were good too.

In the Second World War I served during the whole of its course, having been in the Territorial Army since Munich and having been repatriated from Burma and India home in August 1945 after VE Day and only shortly before VJ Day.

There is no doubt whatever in my mind that the soldiers who served in the First War had very much more horror, discomfort and hardship and immeasurably (on average) more danger than the soldiers in the Second World War. The thought of spending week after week and sometimes month after month in wet or cold mud in horrible unsanitary trenches under constant fire is something which must have been very difficult to endure. Remember that they had no DDT or any other effective insect control. I think that the discipline and responsibility of officers and non-commissioned officers as well as the phlegmatic doggedness of the British soldier must have enabled them to suffer through what must have been almost unendurable.

In the Second War there were occasions when soldiers, sailors and airmen suffered great hardship and had to use and fall back upon enormous powers of endurance, but not on the scale of the First World War, at least in so far as I have been able to form a judgement.

I have mentioned before that I was disappointed that the Great War had finished before I was old enough to take part in it. I did at one time consider the possibility of joining the Royal Navy or the Royal Air Force but my sight was not good enough so that I rather abandoned the idea and it was not until Munich and the appeasement of Hitler that I realised there must be a war in the fairly near future and I joined up as a Gunner with the 252 (City of Oxford) Battery in what I think was the 18th Heavy Ack Ack Regiment RA. It was good fun and we had a wonderful time at camp, at drills and always amongst a very good selection of young men in Oxford.

When it became obvious that there must be a war we were called up as Territorials on 4 August 1939 and after a period of training at Boarstall Heath and Clapham Common we went down to Cleave in North Cornwall to have some Ack Ack shooting practice where we were supposed to actually fire these guns. It was thick fog for the whole time that we were there so we could not see to fire at anything with any degree of safety. As we had to come back on the last day of our training and the fog had still not lifted we were allowed to fire into the fog in the general direction of the sea so that at least we could say when we went to defend London we had actually had firing practice.

So it was that we went to London and my Battery position was in East Dulwich right on the golf course where I spent the first week or so sleeping on the concrete floor of the locker room. Concrete is awfully hard on the hip and proved to be the lesson once again that it is better to have a hip pillow than a head pillow if you are sleeping hard or rough.

War was duly declared. The sirens went and we manned our guns for everyone expected that there would be an immediate heavy air raid on London. As you know nothing happened.

Early in September 1939 I was pulled out of the Battery with about six or eight others including friends Paddy Powell, Horsborough, Bill Bullock and a few others who were to be the nucleus of a new light Ack Ack regiment which was being formed in Oxford with Colonel Ian Twisledon-Wykeham-Ffiennes. He was a fine man and became a personal friend. He later became Lord Saye and Sele and Edith and I visited him at Broughton Castle.

When I was posted back to Oxford it was as a Lance Bombardier and as such I went into The Mitre bar at lunchtime between some training periods. The next morning the Adjutant told us that we were to be commissioned as soon as the necessary formalities could be completed and in the meantime we were each to take charge of about thirty recruits who were joining up with commendable speed. We were told to put up three stripes as Troop Sergeants and to look after and take responsibility for our troops immediately. So it was as a Sergeant that I next went into The Mitre bar with my friends Max Adamson and Bill Bullock who were both in the same position. The next day we went in as Sergeant Majors because they had needed our stripes for the old soldier recruits who were to become our NCOs. Our meteoric promotion continued when our commissions came through and Messrs Adamson had made our uniforms in anticipation and we duly graced The Mitre bar as Second Lieutenants. This promotion was rather fun but my next promotion to Captain after only about two months' commissioned service was, I felt, rather too much. However, our Battery had an establishment of five captains and I was to be one of them so it was as Captain that I next called into The Mitre bar only a month or so later.

Things steadied down a bit then and I was not promoted to Major until November 1940 when I was posted to a new Regiment in Hampshire on the Isle of Wight where I had a most interesting command as Battery Commander of the 89th LAA Battery. My armament consisted of a troop of Bofors at Ventnor Down, a 3' gun at each of Cliff End, Needles, Bembridge, All Sands Fort, No Man's Fort and a Lewis gun at Brigade Headquarters at Yarmouth. As it took me at least a day to get round my Battery positions I was in a fortunate position and was able to dodge my visiting Colonel and Brigadier fairly easily if I wanted to do so. These were boring times but we had some fun and one little incident has always stuck in my mind. It was a brigade order that whenever a senior visiting officer arrived at a gun site they would take posts and when the visiting officer actually arrived at the gun positions the No. 1 would order detachment rear. He would double smartly to the visiting officer and report his name, the number of men in the detachment and any other information relevant to his gun position. One of my best Sergeants was a dear old gentleman's gentleman named Marks and he went through the drill perfectly and doubled up to Brigadier Revell-Smith who was visiting and said: 'Sergeant Marks, Sir – eleven men on parade, two sick and we have sunk the *Bismarck*.' He had just got the news over their wireless that the Royal Navy had sent *Bismarck* to her watery grave to the delight of everyone. There was not really very much to cheer about but that was one thing that brought a laugh and a cheer together.

It was very interesting to note how different commanders of different grades had different whims and fads and methods. One would always look up the spout of your gun and complain of a bird's nest in it. Another would make sure that all the men's bootlaces were properly done up. Another would give orders that boots should be polished and the next would counter the order by saying that they must be dubbined. I was amazed one morning when the dubbined boot order was changed to polished boot order and within an hour all but one troop of my Battery had their boots highly polished. I found that exasperated by the changes in the order they had decided to polish their boots and when they were not walking out they left them unpolished so that they looked as though they had been dubbined.

Then there were the swill-tub men whose first question was 'Where is your swill tub?' I first heard of this one when serving under Major Amery at Dulwich where he encountered an early representative of the swill-tub Brigade. Amery knew this Brigadier's propensity and was walking down towards the kitchen when he noticed that one of the swill tub's lids was off, which was quite a crime. Amery, who was a brilliant talker, immediately started to expound on the beauties of London as seen from East Dulwich. From our position we were high up and could see a number of London's famous buildings. He took the Brigadier along at a great speed pointing out one landmark after another and when they had got past the cook houses and the offending swill tub the Brigadier turned to Amery and said, 'I see you saw it too, Amery.'

VOYAGE TO INDIA

I HAVE BEEN ABLE to read reams of correspondence passing between my parents or, more accurately, Bunny's letters to Edith. It appears that she was anxious to keep everything, whereas Bunny had little or no alternative but to avoid carrying excess baggage round the world. We do, however, have a letter from Edith dated 2 December 1941:

> *Thank you so very much for a wonderful weekend. I was so pleased to be able to come to you again before our separation. I love you with all my heart. I am sure we are the only two people who know what real love is.*
>
> *It was so sweet of you to send me a letter card straight away. I got it this morning. I knew why you didn't say much about the children and I was so grateful.*
>
> *I begin to feel that perhaps you won't be gone from me for quite so long as I had at first thought. I shall long for your letters or cables and you know you will always be in my thoughts. You know that I am yours absolutely and entirely and always shall be. I too know that you are mine and mine alone. We shall always have our love to cheer us. Goodbye my precious and please take every care of yourself. Yours for ever and ever, Edith.*

On 4 December 1941 in a letter to Edith posted from Holywell, Flintshire:

> *I love you darling. I have meant all my promises and I shall come back to you.* Later on in the letter he continues: *I haven't seen Bernard again and don't expect I shall now. Today I had to send someone to Leicester and told him to call and see Jack for me and ask him for a box of cigars.*

Whether or not he got them I do not know but knowing Jack's generosity I expect he did.

From here on the correspondence clearly involves the censor although in some of the more personal letters I note that the censor was none other than Bunny. It was clearly a secret as to where the ship that was boarded in Liverpool was going and by what route and when. In places pieces of the text have been deleted and addresses torn out etc. The other problem is that so many letters were written, some of them undated, and I have tried as best I can to sort out the order. Particularly difficult are the times when more than one letter has been sent on the same day.

We know now that on 7 December 1941 the ship was underway and Bunny wrote:

I think I shall enjoy our voyage unless the weather is bad. If so I rather doubt my ability to avoid being seasick. It has turned cold and the wind is rather fresh so my misgivings are increasing and I shall no doubt make presents to the fishes of the excellent food I am getting. What I do not know is the name of the ship.

The next letter clearly written at sea was dated 15-18-21 December 1941:

The sea is calming down and I have won my battle against seasickness. The night before last even the crew admitted it was rough and I feel that as I survived that I shall be alright. I should like to have you with me on this ship, my darling. I can't tell you the name of the ship but she did go in for holiday cruising and after the war we may be able to go on her together. We are out of the real danger zone for aircraft.

The above is written with a most beautiful pen I have bought for you. Don't judge the pen by the writing. It has a fine nib and I purposely press very lightly so as not to affect it for you but I felt I must write with it before I send it. It is a real Parker and I was fortunate in getting one of the last two from the ship shop. I think you will agree that it is a very pretty one too. It may be in this letter but I won't send it unless I find that it is reasonably likely to get to you. I wonder where I shall be when I get your next letter. I know it will be a sweet one and I know it will be something more for me to treasure.

The weather is getting warmer everyday we go south and soon I expect we will be getting into shirts and shorts as a proper garb. I hope too that we shall be able to sleep on deck. The cabins are of course stuffy because of the very very strict black-out. It is a very serious offence even to smoke out of doors – I should say on deck. One is told that at sea the glow of a cigarette can be seen for a mile. I rather like the life aboard ship although it is hopelessly incomplete with you not being with me. How I should love to be seeing these new things with you. All the beautiful things I see, the phosphorescence of sparks and sparkles in the lashing foam, the blue and silver evenings and the dawns and sunsets all seem somehow fulfilled by our love so I wonder if you understand me, my darling, I mean that when I see anything beautiful my brain thinks of you and it together and it becomes a thing of holiness as well as beauty. Dearest, darling always love me and we will both look forward to that marvellous reunion and joy.

What of the war? It looks goodish to me at the moment in spite of the Japs' progress and the loss of our two fine ships, Prince of Wales and Repulse. But there will I have no doubt be all sorts of changes before you get this letter. I hope the Russians may have pushed back the Hun to his own soil by then and that we have mopped up the whole of North Africa. This letter will be taken off somewhere along the West African coast and I expect may possibly get to you in two to three weeks' time. I will try and send you a cable for Christmas but I don't think it will be possible as wireless silence has to be preserved and it is most unlikely that we shall be going ashore for some long time.

We are having marvellous food and I am trying everything gradually. The nicest new thing that I have is a sweet corn fritter with syrup. It is like the hottest and sweetest fried doughnut you have ever had with lashings of golden syrup over it. I think you can buy packets of sweet corn flour; if so I should get some and try it.

I am getting quite a lot of bridge but it is rather difficult to get a table as there are so many other officers aboard and a lot of them like to play.

Boxing Day 1941.

I hope you had a good Christmas. I wonder if you saw any of the family. I expect the petrol problem made it difficult for Bessie to see you but I know she would have called if she could. At one place we called at the Bum boats came alongside selling fruit and other things such as raffia baskets. It was most amusing hearing the troops exchanging banter and bargaining with the natives. Throughout the voyage we have had a noble escort and haven't seen anything at all of the enemy.

8th February 1942.

We are all very fit and expecting to move soon. I think none of us will be sorry; because we are birds of passage it is not easy to settle down. Poona where we have arrived is rather disappointing though I find the native bazaar interesting though a trifle hummy. We are all however rather broke following the initial expense of a new place. It is extraordinary money seems to go on nothing or almost nothing. I am rather disappointed with the flowers but there are some really fine creepers with mauve closely packed flowers but the others are rather ordinary. Perhaps they will impress me more in the summer. Isn't it strange to have a winter temperature of 92 degrees in the shade and difficult to imagine what it would be like in the summer. So anything over 105 degrees is unusual so I am told that it won't be too bad unless we have to go to an exceptionally hot place. The worst part of the climate is the dust and when we move in column it becomes so thick that it is like moving in a very dirty smoke screen. We have goggles and dust masks so it is not too bad. I must try to get a parcel sent to Richard for his birthday. How awful to post a parcel in February to try to make sure it arrives by June.

What of the war? Not too good at the moment I am afraid but I am sure the Jap will overstep himself just as I believe the Boche has in Russia. The whole thing I think will end very suddenly but I am afraid it won't be just yet. Our men are fit and well and the morale of my own men very high. My men are looking forward to going into action but we don't know of course if and when we ever shall. I expect we shall have to do our share in due course.

The food is good and well cooked but the smell of India is sweet and sickly and at the same time musty. It seems to get into everything and leaves a slightly oily taste which I am told has something of its origins in betel nuts which the natives chew. I hope it isn't that they spit on their hands while kneading the bread. The traffic is cars, tongas and bullock carts. I haven't yet seen an elephant. The tonga is a little trap drawn by a pony and driven by an unusually dirty Hindu. He sits facing the way you are going and his two passengers sit behind looking back. The horse is intermittently very rude and the smell is a concentration of that which I have previously described. So concentrated is it that I literally hold my nose to avoid being sick. The bullock carts are rather nice and the bullocks very docile and apparently friendly. The natives seem to treat their animals reasonably well and the sacred bulls are allowed to wander where they will even though it means allowing them into and out of shops. This does not seem to give them immunity from a good belting with a stick to hurry their progress.

We have about sixty camp followers to look after our lines and I had such fun in the absence of the Colonel in trying to run them to earth and nail them to particular jobs. It is awfully difficult because they will not do any job but their own. The beestis (Gunga Din was one) will look after the ablution benches and clean them by swilling them with water but will not use a broom or brush because that would make them sweepers – a lower grade. Then there are dry sweepers who sweep the roads and paths and wet sweepers who clean the lavatories. The lavatories, even in the best bungalows, are commodes and a good sweeper will wait outside for you to finish and then rush in to do the emptying. I have yet to learn the reason for this continued primitiveness.

The Battery is settling down well and we have one of our first real chances to polish it up a bit. They look like soldiers already and I think I shall get more and more proud of them as time goes on. I was walking along main street Poona today and happened to look into an open drain and there saw two huge rats taking no notice of anyone but very intent on some refuse they were eating. Plenty of dogs were about who were probably unattached and thought it would be kind to live and let live. The animal and bird life is very interesting. There are monkeys but I have seen no wild ones yet and Marmosets and little stripe-backed squirrels all over the place. The prettiest bird I have seen was a big chap like a Jay with very brilliant colouring of kingfisher shades. I saw a huge butterfly yesterday but he would not settle so I could not get a really good look at him.

EARLY NOTES NARRATED BY BUNNY (PART II)

IN DECEMBER 1941 WHILST still very green I went abroad as Major Second in Command of the 24th Light AA Regiment RA. We left Liverpool in December 1941 when Bernard was able to get down to the dock to see me off. We had a wonderful trip to Freetown in a large convoy going due west across the Atlantic before turning south. We had Christmas Day in Freetown harbour with plenty of beer and very hot weather. We then called at Cape Town where I saw the *Queen Mary* and the *Normandy*. We then went to Durban where we stayed a few days and then off again, thinking we were going to the Persian Gulf and thence to stop the Germans coming through the Caucasus, who had by then invaded Russia.

I am not quite sure where we had got to when the disaster of Pearl Harbour occurred. Because of it we were diverted to India and there we landed at Bombay and spent a few weeks in Poona before going into Calcutta where we defended Alipor airfield and I met the first fighter VC of the war (Squadron Leader Nicholson). We made friends with him and his splendid second in command whose name was Cary and whose chest was smothered in fruit salad.

I had occasion to visit a number of places in India out on training courses or reconnaissance before we actually joined up with our fighting Division (7th Indian Division) at Ranchi before moving down into Arakan in 1943. I liked India very much. I was fascinated by the people and regretted that I could not talk to them in their own language. I only learned a few words of Urdu but enough to discomfort a taxi driver in High Wycombe years later. He was obviously an old soldier who knew a few of the swear words that I also knew. When I got into his cab he was swearing in Urdu and I surprised him by telling him a new one.

It was sometimes incredibly hot in India but I was lucky to be never stricken with dysentery or malaria. Indeed, I do not think I was ever sick the whole time I was in India and Burma, which was for very nearly four years.

It was between our Arakan campaign and our movement up to Kohima before the advance into central Burma and down for our last campaign that I first met George Hodgson (later Canon Hodgson and the Vicar of Silverton in Devon.) He was a great friend of the family and the officiating priest at my daughter Rosemary's marriage in 1969 at Old Headington Church.

We were in training at a camp not far from Ranchi and we were without a Padre. I went into the Officers' Mess Basha hut where we used to help ourselves and sign chits. There was a long lank figure standing there disconsolately. There was no one else in the hut at all and I asked him who he was. He replied, 'Your new Padre.'

I said, 'No one told me you were coming nor did I know that we were getting a new Padre.'

To this he replied, 'Well, I am here.'

I then said, 'I wonder if I might offer you a drink.'

He said, 'Yes, you may.' We had a drink, followed immediately after by another one and we became firm friends. I don't think anybody could have been served by a better man nor a better Padre.

Commanding about a thousand British troops in an unusual and difficult country is bound to produce problems of all kinds for the Commanding Officer. I always consulted people when I could and on any question of psychology it was always George that I turned to. I was a great chap for Battery Commanders' conferences and when it was a question of a decision which affected the whole Regiment I would also invite the Padre, the REME Attached Officer, the Quartermaster and any one else who might be able to give a helpful opinion. In the Army you are supposed to make quick decisions and so you should; I did so when there was no time to think it out and get the benefit of other people's opinion. But when you have time then I think you should use it before committing yourself to a decision which may be wrong. I found that a lot of Commanders took pride in their ability to make quick decisions and so sometimes made bad ones when they might otherwise have arrived at the correct answer by taking time and consultation.

When we joined the 7th India Division I gradually got a reputation throughout the Division of being on the ball. I admit to a certain amount of low cunning and I was always trying to beat the pistol. I would cheat in any way I could for the benefit of the Regiment or the Division or against the enemy. The Regiment had the reputation of always getting the best place for its camps and bivouac areas. We always seemed to achieve and maintain our creature comforts. I had been taught very early in the war by a Brigadier that 'any bloody fool can be uncomfortable.' So I passed that message on in all the units with which I was later associated. One thing I would not allow was any form of dishonesty which deprived other British troops or the poor and distressed natives.

I have never been fond of firearms of any kind. We were brought up by our father to have a very healthy respect for the dangers of firearms and he would never allow us to point a gun at anybody whether it was loaded or not – not even toy guns. I still go cold when recalling how near to tragedy I was on one occasion. In India, whether in Calcutta or one of the training areas, we were ordered always to carry our revolvers with us and to have no round in the first chamber so that an accidental discharge of the weapon would not result in a bullet being fired. We were very short of ammunition but on one occasion we were out in Lohardaga training area when the Colonel (I was then 2 i/c) gave orders that we were to have some practice shooting with our revolvers. We were each allowed to use five rounds and then we would be issued with new ammunition to refill. We all knew that the first chamber had nothing in it and we were told to go off and make our own arrangements for practice. I decided to clear the empty chamber and then to fire at a piece of wood in a pond on the banks of which we were standing. I was about to pull the trigger without paying attention to where the gun was pointing and then I remembered the old teaching that 'a gun is always loaded so never point it at anybody.' I aimed at the piece of wood and pulled the trigger and to my astonishment the gun went off and I found to my surprise that although I had owned and carried the gun for a year or more I had never known that the chamber revolved anti-clockwise instead of clockwise. I had actually carried this loaded revolver about with me for over a year with the last chamber being the empty one instead of the first.

One could go on talking about incidents which happened during the war but I think they might be boring to my readers so I will try now to remember little incidents which could be of interest.

When we were relieved, having defeated the Japs, and when the pass was re-opened one of the first people to come through was the Supremo, Lord Louis Mountbatten, and we quickly organised at his direction a parade for me to introduce my officers. I started off well enough because I had got all my officers on the first wing of the square and then I came to the others and was lucky with two or three and then I got stuck: although I knew the man's face I had no idea what his name was and at my hesitation the Supremo said to the officer, 'Now, what's your name – he does know.' The officer gave his name and they had a little chat; after this each officer picked up the cue and introduced himself to the Supremo and shook hands with him. He then, after the informal parade, stood on a little soap box and called the officers all around him and then told us the stories of war and his meetings with Uncle Joe (Stalin) Roosevelt and Winston Churchill and how it was that he had battled to get material for us in Burma but that everything was being prepared for the second front and they had agreed the first priority for that theatre of war to our detriment.

He said that we would soldier on and that we would get everything that he had promised to get for us. As evidence of this he reminded us that we had been fed and supplied with everything by air over the last three weeks when we had won a battle which in the history of war would rank as one of the most important that had ever been fought.

In about August or September 1943 I had taken over command of 24th Anti-Tank Regiment from Jack Kirton who was a regular and a very fine soldier. I did not find it easy to get on with him but I learnt a tremendous lot from him and can honestly say that I would not have been able to hold my command unless I had had the extra knowledge and experience of serving under him for about year.

18. General Messervy with Bunny

It was matter of great pride to me to take my Regiment into a new Division, especially the 7th Indian Division which was commanded by General Sir Frank Messervy, and I very soon got to know everyone in the Division and I think my Regiment was well thought of. My policy was to do everything I could and if one was not too busy to volunteer for any sort of odd job which was going and that we should do anything and everything we could for the benefit of the Division. It could not be said that we were busy in the first months after we joined our new Division because the Japs had no aircraft to speak of, except for the very high flying planes which we could not reach, and we had no tanks. However, we moved with the Brigades - usually a Battery under Commander of Brigade and dealt with all manner of different types of job to the advantage of the 7th Indian Division. Apart from doing the odd jobs we provided ground defence for the Division and manned an out-board motor boat patrol down the tidal chaungs between Tang Bazar and Moundraw. We performed a reconnaissance on the Naf Peninsular with a troop. We established a rest camp at Elephant Point on the Indian Ocean with only ten to fifteen miles within the Jap positions. It was there that Vera Lynn came down and sang to us and everyone was delighted that she had the courage to do so and her charm was indubitable and her effect on morale was amazingly good. Some thought that it would be bad for morale for Vera Lynn's sentimental songs to be heard by men thousands of miles away from the people they loved but the reverse was the effect. It somehow seemed to give the men a feeling that they still mattered at home and the words proved to them that their wives were being faithful at home.

Another odd piece of morale building was unintentional. It was leaked out much to the annoyance of High Command that the 14th Army in Burma was known in England and the English newspapers as 'the forgotten army'. Our command thought that the troops would hate this but actually they loved it and talked of themselves and wrote home with the title 'forgotten army' at the top of their notepaper.

To go back to the odd jobs that we did: we ran a jeep convoy over the Ngakeydauk Pass – known universally as the Okeydokey Pass. This was a splendid and perilous job which we undertook and indeed we volunteered for it. It should be explained that my establishment entitled me to about fifty jeeps – it might have been more - and the only vehicles for which the Pass could be constructed immediately was for the jeep with its four wheel drive narrow wheel base and manoeuvrability. The Sappers constructed this track and eventually we were able to get a jeep through. I think the first jeep was driven by Staff Sergeant Rattew. The last I heard of him was at a garage in the Lyndhurst Road in Bournemouth. The track was built around the contours through the Pass and sometimes there was a drop of seventy five to one hundred feet 'down the cud'. It needed a great deal of nerve to drive it but my drivers became so skilful that they were able to do it whilst maintaining a good speed. Our first job was to deliver rations to a Battalion of the Queens in our Division and, unfortunately, to return back over the Pass not empty but loaded with the wounded, some of them stretcher cases following an attack. We had something like forty drivers running the jeeps to and fro along this track which was four or five miles of the most difficult driving you can imagine. We recruited the drivers from volunteers with a preference for London taxi drivers and civilian lorry drivers. They were a magnificent lot and I cannot speak too highly of their skill and devotion to their difficult job. About ten years after the war, when I had my leg in plaster from an Achilles tendon operation, I was standing disconsolately outside the law courts in London, trying vainly to attract a taxi. Suddenly, a taxi going the other way swung round in the road and stopped right by me. The driver said, 'Jump in, Colonel. Where do you want to go?' He took me to Paddington and I chatted with him all the way through the window between us and when I got to Paddington I had the greatest difficulty in getting him to take my fare.

Eventually, the whole of the Regiment passed through the Pass, the track of which had gradually been strengthened and widened so that large vehicles could make it. Indeed, later on it took the Sherman tanks of the 25th Dragoons. I established my Regimental Headquarters just through at the end of the Pass at Sinzewar and was instrumental in the preparation of the defences for the Administrative Box in command of which I was put. We had all sorts of troops – Clerks, RASC, Sappers, Mule Remount Companies, a troop of 8th Belfast Heavy Ack Ack, two of my own Batteries, one manning Bofors, and the other also with anti-tank guns, the bridge building section, Brigade Headquarters, a Field Ambulance with operating surgeons and many others. Our three fighting Divisions, 33, 89 and 114 went through us right across the plain northwest of the Mondur Buthidaung Road which went through the famous tunnels and our furthest Brigade was alongside the Kalipansin River.

Early in February 1944 somehow or other a strong Japanese force of, I think, two Brigades went right through 114 Brigade during the night. There was confusion and they did not understand that they were enemy troops whose mules clattered through their lines. In a few days our Division was completely surrounded by an approximately similar force of Japs who had learned that the British Army always fights to open its line of communication. Unfortunately for the Japs, that policy was not acted upon. For the first time the Division was supplied by air during a battle in which it was completely cut off from its bases. The battle lasted for about twenty-five days starting in February 1944 and it was the first occasion that Japanese troops were beaten on the ground in the war. I was in command during the early days of the battle and then Geoff Evans (Brigadier) who commanded one of the Brigades of the 5th Indian Division took over from me and brought with him a magnificent Battalion – the 2nd West Yorks. Geoff Evans later became the Divisional Commander and then rose to the rank and position after the war of CIGS. He was a very good soldier and very alert.

THE BATTLE OF THE BOX

AFTER THE BATTLE OF THE BOX Bunny was asked by his General, Sir Frank Messervy, to prepare a narrative as to his part in the battle and a copy of such account has been found. It does not, however, give the full picture. In addition, it is accepted that Bunny had to speak on Air India radio but what he actually said is not available. It is believed that a copy of the transcript may be in the Imperial War Museum. However, on 24 February 1941Bunny wrote a letter to Edith which has been heavily censored and unreadable. The remainder is as follows:

I can't remember what I said in my last letter and I am not sure if it will have got through so I will give you all the news perhaps again. For nearly three weeks now we have been fighting a battle against the Jap who has been trying hard to eliminate us having succeeded in cutting our line of communication and getting all round us. We have already spoilt the whole of his very optimistic plan which he fondly imagined would completely liquidate us and the rest of the troops in the Arakan. We get supplies and newspapers by plane and from the latter it seems that we have got a very good chit from above, by we I mean our Division, but the Regiment has done its full share and I think I have done my personal share too. I got a very slight wound – a lump of shell in my arm while I was stopping the spread of fire in one of our ammunition dumps and had it cleaned up under anaesthetic. That was about five days ago or so and I wrote my last letter when still under the influence of the anaesthetic which merely makes one feel quite tiddly. I remember telling you in my letter that I was still a wee bit drunk.

25th February '44.

The pass has been opened and everything now should be much easier. Above all one is so relieved to see the poor wounded evacuated. Poor chaps some of them have been lying untreated and sometimes under fire for over 3 weeks. The doctors have been simply magnificent and have established their operating theatre again. Their first hospital was overrun by Japs one night and the dirty little swine killed most of the officer patients in cold blood. They killed many of the men too and several of the doctors. Fortunately most of the doctors were saved to carry on their good works. I cannot speak highly enough of them. It has also been most hectic and although we are not yet completely out of the wood we have definitely won a victory and hope to go on to others. I think I once told you that the 14th Army would rival the 8th. So it has already and will go on to further success. I have lost many good men and a fair few wounded but we are carrying on with confidence now of our ability to undergo the strains and trials of battle. For myself, darling, I am glad that I can do my share when it is necessary without undue windup. It is harrowing sometimes but the morale of all the division is very high. We are a mixed lot: British, Scotch, Irish, Gurkha, Punjabi, Sikh, Madrassi and all sorts and they have nearly all done well. One has seen many acts of heroism and some of my men should get decorations for their share in the victory. Peter and in fact all the officers are well though four of us have minor wounds.

It must have been a very annoying thing for the Jap when he found that we were not going to withdraw. He captured Div HQ and I expect thought that we would all 'bargo'. Instead most of Div staff got away and linked up with me when everything started gradually to function again and the defences of the Box held and in the last three weeks has killed over three hundred Japs…………Last night was quieter and only the odd Jap seemed to be around. We had this morning a message of congratulation from the Army Commander and it seems that 7 Divs name is very high everywhere. We had a press correspondent last night who was told officially that we had shot down ten Jap planes. We have also hit a good many more so you may read or have read about us in that connection in the papers. It is not quite so tense now but we must be awfully careful not to slacken off.

Did I tell you that Ted (Teddy Cole) was coming down to see me. It is a good job he wasn't here just before the battle because he would have been quite unable to get back and his old Colonel would have been simply furious. Perhaps he will be able to get over now but I doubt it very much as all available space will be wanted on the convoys coming over the pass.

My arm continues to make good progress. I only have a bit of sticking plaster over it now.

There had been difficulty in communication and the 14th Army were generally referred to as the 'forgotten army' which will be mentioned in other parts of this book. It seems that reference to the Air India radio was that Bunny spoke shortly after 0815 hours on 12 March 1944. It is assumed that he did not read out details of the other theatres of war but merely the piece relating to the 14th Army which says as follows:

'AND NOW BLIMEY WE ARE ON THE NEWS.'

14th Army: After nearly 2 weeks bitter fighting the Japs have been brought to a standstill east of the Mayu Range. Some Japs may be in danger of being cut off between our troops. This position is due entirely to the stubbornness of our troops who inflicted far more casualties on the Japs than they sustained themselves. In the Taung Basar area Allied Troops refused to retreat. All this made the Jap dream of seeing our Army scuttling back across the Ngakeydauk Pass fade away.

My enquiries do not reveal exactly what was said on the broadcast but a letter from Bunny dated 16 March 1941 is helpful and the relevant part reads as follows:

I am afraid, my dear love, that you will have had a very lean time for letters just recently but by now I am hoping you will have had my after the battle cable and letter and will know that I am alright. Thank you, my darling, for your lovely letters. The last I had were the two of 28th February and up to then you obviously hadn't heard of the battle which I learn hit the London headlines on 1st March. There is such a lot to tell you. I was ordered to go to broadcast about the show and was duly flown to Calcutta having prepared my script with the aid of a newspaper man, had it censored and nerved myself to the ordeal. I was told I should make a record which would later be put in the programme. When I got there I found I was, after all, to do a direct broadcast and was a wee bit frightened. I did it and it wasn't bad for I heard it played back to me two minutes later, they having taken a recording as I broadcast. It is simply amazing how one does not know one's own voice. What one hears when talking is so affected by the vibrations inside one's face that it sounds nothing like the voice which someone else hears. I had no idea my voice was like it is and I am not sure whether I like it or not.

You will want to know, my love, whether the broadcast is being relayed to England. I tried hard to find out but couldn't but it is possible I am afraid that it may have been done without your knowing it. I suggest you write to the BBC and ask them whether the talk on the 7th Indian Division victory in the Arakan by a senior officer of the Division from Calcutta on the 12th March has been or is going to be broadcast or relayed by the BBC. If it was given I am afraid you would have missed it as infuriatingly enough nearly all my own men did because of a mistake in notification of the time. However, it was re-published practically verbatim in the Statemans and I am sending the original script to you by air mail in a day or two.

It was rather fun but I should have liked it much better if I had thought there was the remotest chance of your listening in to me.

You are so sweet – your letters I love and I can't tell you what a kick I get from reading them. Oh, my darling, how marvellous it will be when we meet again – it will be simply wonderful.

Shells are simply whistling overhead just now but they are all going the right way. Mr. Nippo is getting another pasting.

The Narrative:

In August 1943 the 24th LAA/A Tank Regiment RA which I commanded was posted to the 7th Indian Division and then in its training at Ranchi and in process of moving to Arakan. The regiment consisted of 2 LAA(86th and 491) Batteries, each of twelve x 40 mm guns and two A Tank Batteries (205 and 284), each of twelve x 57mm guns.

The Regiment moved to Arakan between September and November 1943 where the AA Batteries were deployed on L of C tasks and 284 A Tank Battery RA in an anti-boat role at Redwinbyin, Nhila and on the barge Durham in the Naf River. The Regiment also provided river patrols in outboard-engined patrol boats covering the Naf River and the Pruma Chaung and were sometimes called in to evacuate casualties by water from the then forward areas to Bawli.

On 20 November 1943 the Ngakyedauk Pass was opened for the controlled running of jeeps and the Regiment formed a jeep convoy of approximately forty vehicles which carried supplies over the Pass to 89 Brigade who were advancing southwards east of the Mayu Range. This convoy continued to run until the Pass was opened to all vehicles on 31 December 1943 by which time all three Brigades of the 7th Indian Division and most Divisional troops were at East Mayu, having been relieved of West Mayu by the 5th Indian Division. The total amount of supplies carried over the Pass during the period between the 20th of November and the 31st of December was over two million lbs. and 902 casualties were evacuated back, of which 129 were stretcher cases including two Jap Prisoners of War.

By 17 January 1944 the whole of the Regiment had moved to East Mayu to join the Division. The AA Batteries deployed and on the 20th and 26th of January 1944 Jap fighters attacked part of the Divisional area and on each occasion one was shot down and a number of hits were scored. At this time and since the 8th of January I was personally commanding the 7th Indian Division Admin Base (sometimes called the Admin Box) and my responsibility was to organise and co-ordinate its defences. I held a conference of all Unit Commanders within the Box and their positions on the ground with the position of those units who joined us on the 5th and 6th of February.

Later on I sent a circular letter to all Unit Commanders confirming their orders and the principles upon which they would fight if and when the occasion arose. The base was taken over by 15th Indian Corp on the 1st February but I remained in command.

Where the Pass emerges east of the Mayu Range is a flat area of paddy fields bounded to the west by the main Mayu Range. These are also bounded to the northwest corner by the valley which runs up to Shwechaing to the north by jungle-covered hill features, and to the east by the ridge of hills in the centre of which is Pt 315 and which is broken by the east gate where the roads and chaung run through to Ngakyedauk village. They were also bordered in the southeast corner by a valley which runs down to Tatmin Chaung (known as Tank Valley) and Mid South by the ridge of hills, the northern tip of which is the feature known as Artillery Hill and the southwest corner by the valley which runs parallel to the main Mayu Range and contained 9 Brigade 'B' Echelon. Approximately in the middle of the south part of the

Admin Base plain is a feature known as Ammunition Hill around and extending northwest and northeast where the Corp ammunition dump was situated. All hills are jungle covered and there is some scrub in the middle of the paddy fields which form the plain.

The position on the 4th of February was that none of the hills surrounding the Box were held by our troops for the very good reason that we had no troops with which to hold them and the defence of the various units consisted of their own small unit perimeters linked up when possible with those of adjoining units.

When the news came through of the Japs encircling thrust and his occupation of Taung Bazar the General ordered 89 Brigade to advance and destroy the Japs in the Taung area. In the afternoon of the 4th of February I recalled into the Box my two Batteries of Anti-tank guns from the point 147 Area where in the light of events they were in an exposed position and their loss to the enemy could not be risked. I had received information that the enemy in considerable force was moving in the area of West Badana towards Shwechaing. This suggested probably attacks on the northwest and north boundaries of the Box and I signalled all Admin Base Units to prepare to defend their areas. I also deployed two Anti-tank troops in Infantry roles to reinforce the admin units in covering possible lines of enemy approach and sent one of my officers with the mixed force of Gunners Infantry reinforcements and even a few RAF personnel to establish a strong position on Ammunition Hill.

That evening, Lieutenant Colonel Cree, with 2 West Yorks (less one Company) moved into the Box to safeguard 9 Brigades L of C. 9 Brigade had taken over the right flank of the 7th Indian Division at East Mayu.

Before dawn on the 6th of February heavy small arms and later mortar fire was heard from the direction of Division Headquarters and line communication with Division broke down. R/T communication existed from my RHQ to HQRA 7th Indian

Division and I was still able to speak by telephone with 15 Corps HQ. At about 10.00 hours I spoke to the Corps Commander over the telephone and requested that the Pass be closed at the west end to allow me to send casualties and soft vehicles over and to prevent vehicles coming in to swell the already considerable number of vehicles within the Box. He agreed to this suggestion. I also reported to the Corps Commander the determination of the admin units which I was then commanding to stay put and fight. The Corps Commander told me that Brigadier Evans of 9 Brigade was on his way to assume command. The Brigadier arrived and took over command from me and established his HQ at my command post from which we had established line and in some cases wireless communication with most of the admin units. Just a short while before that a Carrier Patrol of the West Yorks, having contacted the 25th Dragoons who were then supporting 89 Brigade northeast of the east gate, reported that the enemy appeared to be all round the admin base. At about the same time I received a signal from Corps HQ which I at once passed to everyone with whom I was in touch, including all of the admin-based units. I have no copy of this signal but the wording of the signal I sent out was:

'Supreme Commander promises strong and immediate reinforcements. It is essential that every man remains at his post and fights to the last.'

Until about 11.20 hours I remained in R/T communication with HQ RA but they could only tell me that Divisional HQ was being hard pressed by the enemy and it was at about 11.20 hours that a message was received that they were moving to my HQ in the base over the hills. The last thing we heard over the wireless was a voice saying, 'Put a pick through the set.' I then ordered my rear link set to assume BA control and communications were maintained with the other Gunner Units of the Division and with 7th Indian Field Regiment RA who were 15 Corps Troops on that set during the whole course of the battle and were used by the CRA as his own after his arrival. A little later the same morning General Messervy arrived at the command post of the Box with his G staff and his orders to 89 Brigade to concentrate on the Box were passed by my wireless to 136 Field Regiment RA and from them to their FOO with 89 Brigade and by him to the Brigade Commander. We also provided a No. 19 set and operators as a link with 25 Dragoons at whose HQ in Tank Valley the General first established his HQ.

During the 6th February the other Units moved into the Box in a proper and orderly manner. It cannot be denied that there was some confusion but all units responded well to the orders they received as to where to go and what was expected of them. Any confusion that did arise was caused by the unavoidable traffic congestion and to a certain natural excitement among the stragglers from those who had been cut off from Divisional HQ during the attack on it and had come into the Box by the main road. All the guns were brought into the Box and were quickly brought into action; mention will be made of the special uses to which they were later put.

At about 1500 hours the CRA and most of the HQ RA personnel, Lieutenant Colonel Hobson with a number of his Signallers and the A/Q Lieutenant Colonel d'Abice with the ADMS and the bulk of the A/Q and medical staff arrived. My RHQ cooks and batmen performed a lesser miracle of meal production for the multitude. HQ RA was established at the command post.

Carrying out the orders passed over my set to 89 Brigade where the 4/8 Gurkha Rifles (less two Companies) had been cut off and later fought their way over the Mayu Range and back with the relieving force arrived at the east gate of the Box where Battalion HQ was established.

On the morning of the 7th of February the 4/8 Gurkha Rifles were forced off the eastern-most feature which they were holding and the Commander ordered a withdrawal onto features further west. But B Company West Yorks supported by a troop of 25

Dragoons restored the situation and the Gurkha Rifles reoccupied their positions. From then on that end of the 315 Ridge was firmly held and was the scene of many battles between the Gurkha Rifles with their AA and Anti-tank Gunners against the Japs. I was able to keep R/T communication with them through my battery set during the whole of the battle and valuable targets were given from time to time to the CRA. Divisional HQ moved to my – now Brigadier Evans' – command post.

Between the 10th and 23rd of February the Box was attacked nightly at some point or other and some attacks were made in daylight. In one of those, Gunners of 136 Field Regiment RA, 139 Jungle Field Regiment RA and my 284 Anti-tank Battery RA who, in inadequate strength had occupied Artillery Hill, were forced off after a gallant stand in which Battery Sergeant Major Griffiths MM of 284 Battery won the DCM and the hill was recaptured by the West Yorks after the most devastating tank support which can be imagined from 25 Dragoons.

Artillery Hill is only about 150 to 200 yards from the road and other places from which a squadron of tanks were able to bring its fire to bear. They fired their 75 mms at this almost point blank range at a very rapid rate and the percussion bursts of the shells destroyed trees, fox holes and the Japanese with ruthless precision. There was one particular position into which we had seen the Japs go and after several bursts on it I myself saw a Jap attempt to leave and get the few yards necessary to get over the crest and out of danger. As he crawled up these few yards a shell hit him and blew him to pieces. After the 75 mm barrage they fired AP shot and Brownings over the heads of the West Yorks as they went up.

Further special incidents are worthy of mention. There was the attack on 20 Mule Company (one of many) when the company staunchly held its ground and inflicted a number of casualties on the enemy and recovering, I think, eight bodies the next morning. So delighted were these Indian Sepoys – without previous battle experience – that they urged their Commander – Captain Graham - to allow them to go out looking for Japs. They later captured a Jap who was only slightly wounded.

Another battle worthy of particular note was one of the last of the siege. A force of Japs moved along what we called Goldings Chaung at the foot of Artillery Hill towards the Command Post and 9 Brigade HQ. They had to pass defended positions of my 284 Anti-tank Battery commanded by Major G.T. Golding RA and positions of 8 and 65 Mule Companies and the 24 Mountain Regiment Mule lines. In the process a pitched battle developed and in the morning 28 dead Japs were found and three wounded prisoners of war were taken for the loss of 1 officer and four men.

All available weapons were bought into service. For instance, the Divisional Div Ord Field Park as is usual had reserved weapons, particularly Brens and 5 x 3 mortars. These were all issued out where they were most needed and the five mortars were manned and fired by Major J. Thompson RA with his 205 Anti-tank Battery personnel of my regiment with devastating effects.

I have dealt with the general conditions in the Box in my broadcast from *All India* radio on the 12th of March but one side of it which I do not think has been adequately covered by anyone is the support given to our troops in the Box and the casualties inflicted on the enemy by our artillery from within and without.

It will be remembered that 6 Medium Regiment RA; 24 Mountain Regiment; a troop of 8 Belfast NAA Regiment RA and the 12/40 mm guns of my 491 LAA Battery were in the Box during the battle. Outside the Box and all within range were the 136 Field Regiment RA which was in the 33 Brigade Box 7th Indian Field Regiment, which was in a box of its own by Awlynsyin east, and the whole of the 5 Division Artillery on the other side of the Mayhu Range. Fire plans were prepared by the GRA 7th Indian Division (whose HQ was in the same command post as was Brigadier Evans and myself) and counter battery fire was controlled by him; at all times during the day and night artillery fire could be and constantly was brought down from outside to harass and destroy the enemy wherever he could be located and to give defensive fire and support to our own troops. The big guns with us – the 5.5s of the 6th Medium Regiment RA and the 3.7s of the NAA – engaged in counter battery shoots daily, not only at the small battalion and mountain guns which the enemy had in place at the 315 ridge, but also at the 150 and 105 mm guns of the enemy south of the Maungdaw-Buthidaung road which dropped ten to fifteen shells into the Box most afternoons.

As to the direct firing actions taken by 8 Belfast HAA Regiment RA is memorable. Their guns of necessity were within full view of the 315 ridge and one afternoon they were shelled fiercely from that ridge. Two guns were put out of action and a lot of their men were killed and wounded. The flashes of the enemy guns were observed and within a few minutes the Belfasts were shooting them up with their remaining two guns over open sights. Though it was difficult to confirm positive hits, so far as I know no enemy guns fired from those particular positions again. The Belfasts subsequently got both their damaged guns back into action again.

The 6th Medium Regiment RA with their 5.5s also shot over open sights at ranges sometimes as low as two hundred to three hundred yards and my 40 mms engaged on frequent occasions when Japs were seen to be digging in or when a gun flash was seen anywhere within their range.

Another thing which has not been covered, as far as I know, is the AA resistance to the three Japanese air attacks made on the Box; namely, on the 8th, 9th and 13th February; on each of these days between twelve and twenty Jap fighter bombers attacked the great concentration of vehicles, guns and personnel in the confined space of the Box. My regiment's score for this period was twelve enemy planes destroyed and in addition a number of probables and hits. Of these destroyed planes six were destroyed by my 491 Battery and six by my 86 LAA Battery, one troop of which was under the command of 136 Field Regiment RA in the 33 Brigade Box and the other troop of which was with the 7th Indian Field Regiment.

While the battle of the Admin Box was going on the other boxes remained firm. 114 Brigade east of the Kalapanzin had won. 7th Indian Field Regiment RA with D Troop of my 86 LAA Battery RA, some sapper personnel (at times with support from 89 Brigade) had one and 33 Brigade in their Box held firm and were frequently able to inflict casualties on the enemy. L Troop 284 Battery in an Infantry role in a lone exposed position on Tatmin Chaung just north of Tatmin Khali killed eight Japs and captured one. Two of those killed were officers and useful papers were obtained from their bodies. On one occasion one of my AA gun positions (D Troop 86 Battery) in the 7th Indian Field area was attacked by a gun-busting party of about fifty Japs. The battle went on for about an hour and a half and fifteen to twenty casualties had already been inflicted on the enemy for the loss of one of my men when along came a fighting patrol of the KOSBs and the battle cry 'Up the KOSBs' shouted by Major Knox MC followed by their charge routed the enemy who left bodies and a lot of equipment behind. For your immediate information the Brigade consisted of 1 KOSB, 4/8 Gurkha Rifles, 7/2 Punjab, all of whom are mentioned in this or other narratives which you have read.

After the Pass was opened the Divisional advance proceeded and eventually resulted in the capture of Buthidaung, but there was one further attack on the Box when at dawn on the 25th of March a party of Japs infiltrated and 150 of them established themselves on the hills south of the east gate. He was turned off by 4/15 Punjab after having been very considerably weakened by a Company of the 1/11 Sikhs. He left behind him fifty-four dead.

The details of the fight southwards of the 26th Indian Division to our relief would have been dealt with by others. All I know is what I have been told by various people of that Division and great credit seems to be due to them for their difficult and exhausting fighting on the march south. It was the Wilts who were actually first in but it was, I believe, the Lincolns who finally cleared the 315 Ridge which from all accounts contained a Jap HQ and where the Japs had suffered considerable casualties from our guns.

On 15 February 1944 during the Battle of the Box, Bunny was hit by a piece of shrapnel which struck him in the fleshy part of the shoulder. The piece was presented to him at the field hospital and shortly before his death he gave it to his grandson, David Cole, who fortunately still has it so that we have been able to take a photograph for inclusion in this book. The wound itself left no permanent damage and was not as serious as wartime injuries go but Bunny was very lucky. I think we must agree that it must have been very painful.

The following is from a letter that he wrote to Edith:

16 Feb '44 (or so they tell me)   *24ᵗʰ AA/ATK Regt.*

I am writing this when just a little pickled. You see I have been very slightly wounded and had to go under an anaesthetic to have it cleaned up and properly dressed. It is really only a very slight wound. One of the Jap shells – or rather five of them – hit an ammunition dump of ours and I went out with a couple of stout chaps of mine to stop the fire spreading to other dumps. We managed to do so but in the process one of the many explosions popped a bit of shell into the fleshy part of my left arm just below the shoulder. I had a first field dressing on it and we finished the job and saved a fair quantity of ammunition which was a reasonably good thing.

We have been up against it and I think the worst is now over. You may have read in the papers of our battle in which there have been many heroes. I can't speak too highly of my men whose casualties have been reasonably light. Why I am a bit pickled is that the anaesthetic is a drug called 'pentholin' which has exactly the same effect as alcohol and has to wear off. It is rather a pleasant sensation and a very easy way to get drunk quickly. I am told you don't get a 'morning after' feeling – that remains to be seen but I expect that they know. I am proud of my Division and think that we have fought one of the epics of the war. I have had no letter from you for a fortnight because we are cut off at the moment and all our supplies come from air droppings. The first plane which dropped supplies was piloted by the American General commanding the air dropping wing of the Combined Air Forces which is a good show. We have received stirring messages from Lord Louis and others of the big chiefs who have thanked us for holding out as we have. We – I mean our Division – really has done a good job of work I think and I wouldn't want to leave them. Throughout the whole continuing emergency I have been much impressed by the devotion to duty which has been shown and one battalion from the North of England is quite the best I have seen. We are only in wireless communication with the rest of the world and are not yet out the wood but morale is excellent and I have no doubt as to the result. When you get this letter the fact that you get it will prove that communications are again established which will mean that we have won our little battle as win it we shall and you will know that all starts to go better than before.

The War Office apparently sent a telegram on 6 March 1944 (which I do not have) and followed it up with a letter dated the 11 of March which must have caused some concern if it arrived before the above letter. No one at home had told me about it but I was only six and no doubt it was hoped that I could be protected. But I remember walking home with a school friend (John Eddy) who told me that he hoped my father would be alright. News of the wound had obviously been spread by the local grapevine, even if it had not been in the paper.

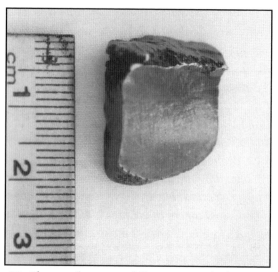

19. *Shrapnel removed from Bunny's shoulder*

Addressed to Mrs E.M. Cole:

Madam,

In confirmation of War Office telegram dated the 6ᵗʰ of March 1944 I regret to have to inform you that a report has been received by telegraph from the Military Authorities in India that your husband, Lieutenant-Colonel R.B. Cole, Royal Artillery, was wounded in action in Burma on the 15ᵗʰ February, 1944, sustaining shrapnel flesh wound to the upper left arm. The report states that your husband was not evacuated from which it would appear that it was not found necessary to admit him to hospital.

If, however, he becomes seriously ill as a result of his wound, further reports will be received by telegraph which will be telegraphed on to you. In the absence of such a communication, it can be assumed that Lieutenant-Colonel Cole, is making normal progress in which event you will, no doubt, hear from him in due course about his wound and progress.

In the meantime communications for your husband should continue to be addressed to him at his unit, where arrangements exist for their redirection if necessary.

Will you kindly notify this office of any change in your address, in case further reports are received.

I am, Madam,
Your obedient Servant,
(signed) T.J. Rayner.

The citation for the DSO is not dated and reads as follows:

THE DISTINGUISHED SERVICE ORDER
Major (temporary Lieutenant-Colonel)
Raymond Buxton Cole (97597)
Royal Regiment of Artillery.

———-

At SINZWEYA in the ARAKAN on the 6th February, 1944, Lieutenant-Colonel Cole was Commandant of the Administration Base when it was first threatened by the enemy. On the arrival of the Commander of an Indian Infantry Brigade to take over the defence of the 'Adm. Box', his local knowledge and assistance was invaluable.

Until the 24th February, 1944, when the NGKEYDAUK PASS was re-opened, his organising ability was most marked. Throughout this period, his coolness, cheerfulness, efficiency and encouragement to the Administration troops, was a great stimulant to the garrison.

On the evening of the 15th February, when part of the ammunition dump was fired by enemy shelling, Lieutenant-Colonel Cole went out with a few men to try and localise the fire. While doing so he was wounded in the arm by flying splinters and lost a considerable amount of blood. Though obviously weak he refused to remain in the Dressing Station and continued to carry out his duties.

The example set by this officer, and his complete indifference to his own safety undoubtedly did much towards the successful defence of the 'Adm. Box'. His conduct throughout was deserving of the highest praise.

He was gazetted on 18 May 1944. The ribbon was presented by Lord Louis in the Box. Throughout his life Bunny was justifiably proud of his medal and wore it with his other medals when appropriate.

The DSO itself was presented by His Majesty King George VI on 10 June 1947.

I remember the day well as I was given time off from school to attend the investiture and was fêted when I went back to school the next day –which was, in fact, my birthday. In Buckingham Palace I remember in particular being allowed to stand up with my mother for the actual pinning on of the medal.

20. Buckingham Palace Ticket

*21. Bunny being presented with his DSO ribbon by
the Supreme Commander Lord Louis Mountbatten*

22. DSO Medal

PETER COLE

IT IS VERY DIFFICULT to put all events in the correct order bearing in mind all that was happening in 1944 but tragedy struck the family on 6 June. My brother Peter (aged three and a half) was on his way to school at Cutteslowe, which meant walking along the Oxford Northern Bypass with his mother and sister, Rosemary (aged four and a half). Suddenly and without warning he ran into the road having, it is thought, seen a friend on the other side of the road. He was struck by a vehicle and death was instantaneous. I well remember the day as I was fetched from school and the fact that Peter had died was explained to me by my maternal grandfather (R.H. Clinkard). As an immature child (aged six) I cannot remember what my immediate reaction was but I suspect it was one of disbelief. I remember seeing a newspaper headline about a week later which said 'Hitler believed to be dead.' And I remember challenging my grandfather that if they could not be sure about Hitler how could they be sure about Peter. My grandparents with whom we lived were devastated by the accident and as I know since all were anxious about my mother and how RBC was to be told.

Mother tried, I believe, to write, and was not able to do so but Dorothy Walsh (Bunny's sister) wrote a letter to him explaining the position. I remember reading this letter many years later. I cannot give the full details but it was quite magnificent and I know a great comfort to both my parents.

My mother had another problem to deal with and that was that my birthday was on 11 of June and I had been promised a party. Many years later a family friend (Mrs. Walby) told me that my mother was magnificent and although she was prone to tears she kept a stiff upper lip and the party was a great success.

The news obviously reached Bunny on the 18 June and he replied with two letters. I am so proud of those letters that I have included them in full as in my view they encapsulate the deep love and concern that each had for the other.

What I discovered during my search was a scrappy piece of paper which accompanied a photograph of we three children which had obviously been carried by RBC whilst he was away and as far as I can tell it is a poem of his own creation.

23. Left to right: Rosemary, Peter and Richard in 1944

My pride and love were they
Three lusty slender saplings
And thou who seeded them
Mary mother tree
My pride three princelings
And then their mother queen

A sapling to another garden taken
A princeling elsewhere gone to grace
My love softly sweetly deeper
For thou who stay and grace this place
Be brave dear heart in thy pride
In those who stay and
In duty still to do
Pride too please God in knowing
Of my love and pride in you.

18th June 44   ***Lt.Col. R.B. Cole RA***
                                              24 LAA/ATK Regt RA
                                                      S.E.A.C.

My dearest,

I have just received Dorothy's cable and my heart bleeds for you, my poor darling, and yearns to comfort you in our dreadful loss. I know nothing of what happened yet but, my sweet love, the detail matters little and my enduring love for you must be a measure of comfort to you and, your knowledge of it I hope will help you as it has helped me to take this blow. I know it will be more difficult for you but, my darling, you must be brave and must not grieve too much – of course you will I know you won't be able to help doing so - what can I say and what else need I say other than that I love you.

I try not to speculate on what happened, but this I must say now for our later peace of mind and as a holy act; if anyone was in any way to blame they must be forgiven and comforted as I forgive them. Darling please do this and know that I mean what I say.

Darling I long to comfort you and I send my prayers and thoughts urgently to you, let all things now be subjugated to your comfort and to ensuring that Richard and Rosemary with their

86

short childish memories are not allowed to be harrowed by poignant reminders of their little playmate.

It is too late to tell you what to tell them – but then I don't know how much they may have seen. Oh darling, perhaps I shouldn't have written all this before I know but I love you, I love you and I am yours and I shall come home to you and comfort you and I shall send my prayers to you and you must be comforted.

Be so brave my darling and God bless and keep you safe. Yours for ever,
Bunny.

20ᵗʰ June 44   **Lt. Col. R.B.Cole RA**
                                                        24 LAA/ATK Regt. RA
                                                        S.E.A.C

My poor dear darling,

I have received Dorothy's and the Doctor's letter and can so easily imagine how you may have been and in spite of cables, may still be torturing your dear kind good and loyal self with 'ifs' and 'might have beens'. Darling, let us get this straight and right now. I can't wait for your first letter to confirm your thoughts but I think I know you so well that I can think as you do.

My love, everything you did was natural and uncareless. The same thing would have happened whoever had been with the little chap who obviously acted on a sudden impulse and one which no one could have foreseen. There is nothing for you to reproach yourself for darling and my faith and love for you is exactly the same as it always has been. We have suffered a blow and we will share it together as we will any buffet that fate gives us in the future. Our love can and must carry us through every trial and even if it had been in any way your fault I would have loved and trusted you just the same because I know you for what you are a fine and splendid woman of great character.

It would be stupid and cruel for me to ask you to forget, but I do implore you, darling, to treasure a memory of the little chap in his happiness and not to taint it with pictures in your mind of the accident. How glad I am he knew nothing and suffered nothing, and he will be as happy where he now is as he was with you even, my darling. Do you know I thought, when I had got over the shock of the news, a very strange thing. I thought how my old father and mother will welcome him. Darling, this letter will make you cry – it is me – but I had to say it all, darling. God bless you darling, go on with your many jobs and don't let yourself be sad. Dearest love to you, bless you darling, I love you so tenderly that it hurts.
Yours forever and ever,
Bunny.

Bunny was never confirmed whereas Mother was, and I always felt that he only went to church when he had to (usually funerals) but having read these letters I have changed my mind and think that he really was a true Christian.

Peter had been killed and Rosemary and I found this fact easier to accept as we grew older but I remember that we both put pressure on our parents that they should have another boy child who would also be called Peter. We did not have to wait long before we were told that Mother was going to have another baby. We were delighted at the news and continued to press for 'Peter'. Our combined efforts must have had some effect because when a boy was born in May 1946 it was explained to us that it would not be sensible to have the same name as this would confuse everyone and the names were agreed as John Peter Oswald Cole.

John, who is nine years younger than me, followed me to The Dragon and then to St Edward's School before being articled to Bunny. It was always recognised by my sister and me that John was spoilt but we accepted it and realised that his brainpower was better than ours! Perhaps it was the top of the milk which was always destined for his cereals.

After passing his solicitor's finals John married Jacky and became involved in serious activity for the benefit of others through charitable work. He joined the Round Table and had the honour of being elected its National President in 1984. Although I had joined the Round Table myself I did not get very involved except at a low level, and it was not until I went to the Annual Conference Dinner/Dance in Margate that I realised the enormity and importance of John's position.

It is generally accepted that he was a great success. As he was also one of our partners we were proud of him and coped in effect for two to three years to enable him to fulfil all his duties.

24. Bunny with John

BERNARD BUXTON COLE

BERNARD WAS BORN ON 10 November 1897 and referred to himself as the 'Jubilee Boy' (Queen Victoria's Diamond). He was a bachelor but a great admirer of the female sex. He was born in Oxford just after his parents moved there upon Oswald's appointment as an Inspector in the Oxford City Police. He joined up in 1914 having lied about his age and enlisted with the Queen's Own Oxfordshire Hussars. He was a bit inconsistent with details of his own record but there is no doubt that he did see service. He used to tell us that his life was saved by his horse which had smashed his kneecap before he was due to go into battle and that the rest of his troop did go into battle but were eliminated. He used to tell us that he was sold to a circus at the age of five. That clearly was Bernard spinning a yarn.

After the war having returned to Oxford he then went to join the Liverpool City Police until his retirement.

During the Second World War he said he was undercover and told us wild stories. One such story was of a visit with another friend to see a sick mutual friend. The fit friend was an undertaker and they kept the pranks going by getting the undertaker to produce a tape measure and use it to assess the length of the sick friend. The 'victim', who was in his sick bed, was told that there was no chance of getting the body out and perhaps it would be safer for him to leave his flat now before it was too late.

Bernard met, in Liverpool, one Kay Day who was highly skilled in the clothes business and very elegant. There is no doubt that Bernard and Kay were extremely fond of each other. Kay was married to someone else but years later got divorced and was free to marry Bernard. Why they did not do so I do not know. It may have been an unwillingness on the part of Kay or a reluctance in Bernard's case to make a decision. In any event they used to see each other often and it would be a regular trip for Bernard (who then lived in Oxford with my parents) to leave on Friday afternoon, drive to Liverpool and return the following Sunday evening. Bernard was working for Ind Coope and Allsopp (the brewers) as a representative. There was always a ritual before his departure. Depending upon the time of year a bunch of flowers would be picked from the garden. Bernard grew sweet peas with considerable skill and they would have been well received in Liverpool. Also, a basket of fruit and vegetables would be prepared with the addition of two or three rotten bananas. I don't know if he actually liked rotten bananas but what he did enjoy was to annoy his greengrocer friends by saying that he wanted 'two or three rotten bananas.' The last item to be put into the car was the folding camp bed.

This ritual continued for some years until when we were in Cornwall on holiday and Sheila was given the task of erecting the camp bed. She unpacked it but could not work out how it actually fitted together. She went into the lounge and asked Bernard if he could explain how it was erected. His reply was swift and, I am sure, honest. He said, 'I am sorry, I do not have a clue.' I remember Bessie was there and it must have taken her hours to stop laughing.

Bernard really was a super chap and we were very sad upon his death. He had lived with my parents for many years until his death and was, I know, completely happy with them, as they were with him. The address at his funeral on 13 July 1972 was prepared by RBC who was originally going to read it but felt that he could not deliver it for fear that his emotions would take over. The Vicar read it:

Bernard was educated at Bedford House School, Oxford and then joined the Liverpool City Police as a boy. When the First World War broke out he came back to Oxford and at the age of sixteen joined the Oxfordshire Yeomanry – QOOH – and you will see that he is honoured today by the colours of his Old Comrades

Association showing the Regiment's Battle Honours which he shared. Some of his old comrades are here today.

After the war Bernard returned to Liverpool and when he retired from the police in 1951 he came home to Oxford and has since shared the home of his brother and sister-in-law first at Green Ridges and then at Southway here in Old Headington. He joined Ind Coope as a sales representative in 1951 and spent eleven happy years with them until he reached the age limit. He made many true friends amongst his colleagues and those he met in business.

He was a kindly friendly man, shy, but with the happiest knack of putting others at ease. He was the soul of discretion and was always ready with gentle wit to steer discordancy into harmony.

He was not an ambitious man and it appeared that his only ambition was to be kind to everyone and make everyone he met into a personal friend.

He died loved by many and without an enemy in the world. May God rest his soul.

Bernard was a member of the Frewen Club (mention of which has already been made) which was one of his regular watering holes where he was able to play snooker, billiards and bridge and also to talk to his many friends. He had the opportunity of becoming the President of the Club which was regarded as a great honour but almost at the last moment he declined. He could be nervous and he did not want too much responsibility.

25. Bernard aged approx. 16 years

26. Cartoon by Jack, 'Trooper Cole has a nasty dream'

27. Bernard and Jack

MARY ELIZABETH HILLSDON (NÉE COLE)

BESS, OR BESSIE, was the eldest daughter of Oswald and Emma. She was born on 14 November 1891 and in later life preferred to be called B. She was my favourite aunt. Perhaps I was biased because she was also my godmother and did everything she could to help me deal with any problems which I had from time to time. She must have been incredibly brave as she chose at a very young age to go to France at the outbreak of war as a VAD. After the war she returned to England and trained as a school teacher. She got a job at Stoke Lyne and married Ted Hillsdon, the son of the local blacksmith. Barry, their son, was born in 1925.

Ted was a man of great skill and charm and he was a perfectionist. He was a very good gardener and would ensure that his garden would be kept neat and tidy although he did not sometimes work at the speed which a large garden demanded. They used to live in Appleford after their retirement and I often went to see them, sometimes on the train but usually by bicycle. We would have lunch and then a chat before I would make my way home. Before I was allowed to leave Ted would ensure that the tyres on the cycle were pumped up to the proper pressure and the brakes were adjusted and that the bike was in first class order.

He demanded perfection from his garden and although B was a great gardener she would normally stay in the flower department, leaving Ted to tend the vegetables. He would work hard on the garden but however long he spent digging he would spend a similar length of time (or so it seemed) polishing his tools and putting them away afterwards. He used an old shaving brush which he dipped into a small bowl of oil and worked on the tools until they shone.

In 1948 at the time of the Olympics in London I was admitted to hospital for a week having been shot under the left eye by an irresponsible youth. The rest of the family went on holiday to the Isle of Wight. So that I could join them for the second half of the holiday Ted met me from hospital, took me home and drove me to Southampton. In fact, it was not much of a holiday because I got violent earache. For the record the pellet went into the gap between the cheekbone and the bottom of the eye ball. I was very lucky not to have lost my sight. I still have the shot behind my eye.

B used to tell of the occasion in France when she went to a party and met a young pilot who told her that he would be flying the following day and that his route would take him over the chateau in which she was based. He arranged to fly over at noon and asked her to be on the lawn in front of the building so that she could wave at him. She was there at exactly the correct time and the small plane duly arrived. She waved and as she watched the plane she saw something white float down and land quite close to her on the lawn. It was in fact a letter written by the pilot and what was perhaps more important was that it had been marked 'by air mail'. B always said that as this was in the early days of the war it was the first air mail letter to be sent. It was a lovely story and she kept the letter until her dying day. Bunny and I, unbeknownst to each other, made enquiries as to the whereabouts of the letter and I was told that Barry, her son, had destroyed it. It is sad that this piece of history is no longer with us.

Bunny left a note which reads:

On one leave Bess brought home an air mail letter in a pouch comprised of two or three lengths of coloured canvas which would attract attention to itself when dropped from a low flying aircraft and the whole with its 'billet-doux' addressed to 'Nurse Bessie Cole, number 9 British General Hospital, Rouen' was duly delivered there to her. Sad to say this super souvenir had been lost. I know that I once had charge of it myself but thought that when Bessie died I gave it to Barry. He says not – so it is a sad mystery.

Tom has the Oak Leaf awarded to Bessie for service as a VAD for four years.

28. Oak Leaf medal

After Ted's death Bessie lived in Hamilton Road, Oxford, within walking distance of her sister, Dorothy, and later on she lived with my parents for the rest of her life.

B died peacefully on 15 October 1967.

29. Jack, Bessie and Bernard
returning after the Great War

THE DOUGHFIG STORIES (BY BESS)

SOMETIME DURING THE 1880s my father Oswald joined the Metropolitan Police and was posted to V (Wandsworth) Division.

There he lived in the section house and one of his friends also living there was Doughfig. Nothing is known of the man's real name or of his subsequent history but he seemed to have been a cheerful if somewhat irresponsible youth.

There are two pleasant and amusing little stories which concern him.

On one occasion he and Oswald were going to Southampton to row in a regatta. They were faced with the prospect of a very early start as they had to be at the station to catch the first train. The provision of breakfast was their own affair so Doughfig produced the bright idea of having breakfast overnight 'to save time in the morning' so, at a late hour, they consumed vast quantities of eggs and bacon and started off in the morning, secure in the knowledge that they had breakfasted well. They won their race with glory.

The second story also concerns Doughfig's prowess as a cook. On Shrove Tuesday he claimed to be the 'world's best pancake tosser'. The first ones were tossed with great success; encouraged by the plaudits of his friends each pancake went higher into the air. Presently, one of the lads spotted that there was an iron bar going across the old fashioned chimney. This resulted in Doughfig being challenged to toss the pancake over the bar. They watched with joy as the pancake sailed into the air – but alas! – it went from their sight and is forever lodged upon some undiscovered shelf.

These stories delighted us as children so I have written them (in 1965) for the younger members of the family who in their turn may have pleasure and amusement from them.

Life in the section house seemed to have been great fun and the young men became good friends. There were none of the luxurious rooms. They shared the austerity of a dormitory and a mess room. A matron cooked them a main meal each day to fit in with their duties and their other meals.

They bought and cooked for themselves either singly or in small groups. It was claimed that a man who was contemplating marriage was easily spotted as he ate jam on his bread without butter.

D.H. SUTCLIFFE

IN 1989 SHEILA AND I were entertained to dinner by friends and one of the other guests was Douglas Sutcliffe. In the course of conversation he let it be known that he had been in Burma during the war and was in the RAF. I told him that my father had been decorated at the Battle of the Admin Box and Doug told me that he had been flying Dakotas and that their task at some stage was to drop supplies into the Box. I did not realise how close he was to Bunny at that stage as my knowledge of the scene was limited. However, I discovered that Doug had written a book about it. Needless to say, we were able to get a copy of the book *Airborne* (published by the Self Publishing Association Ltd). Sheila sent a copy of the book to Bunny and he read it and returned it with his comments:

Ebor House 10ᵗʰ April, 89.

My dear Sheila,

    Many thanks for sending me the very interesting book Airborne by D.H. Sutcliffe. I am & especially must have been grateful to him and his buddies for dropping rations & ammo & mail into our Admin Box while we were cut off in Feb. '44 from our land delivered supplies. They did a good job & I watched them frequently when they were dropping from about 250' & of necessity only a few feet from the fringeing trees. The amazing thing is that it is forty-five years since that all happened.

    I really must get down to my own memoirs around which I might mention that I switched on my TV this weekend and saw and heard Lord Templeman speaking in the House of Lords. He it was in our Box who facetiously asked if I happened to have a pipe of baccy for his 'gaffer' (Brig. Crowther) who was right out and much 'put out'. I was able to do a super magic trick by producing a 2 oz tin of Three Nuns from my battle dress as dropped for me a few days before in Edith's parcel of goodies. Sidney Templeman was then a Major in 89 Brigade of our 7 Indian Division and I have met him several times since in England when he became a Chancery Judge & latterly a Lord of Appeal. I had two solicitors as Battery Commanders in my (24.AA/ATK) Regt. And my adjutant Derek Hodgson is now a full QB Judge whom Richard knows.

Having dealt with the build-up of troops the text on page seventy-three of *Airborne* reads as follows:

On the evening of 4th February 1944 Slim ordered air supply to be made available to the two Divisions (5th and 7th) cut off. My first trip to the beleaguered army was on the 5th. In my log book I simply note is as 'special'. Calvert in reference to the two Divisions' plight simply says 'as they had been placed on air supply their cutting of their road communication was not important.' Such was the confidence that we could perform! These Divisions were encircled and in grave danger from the 5th – 24th February. Several times the perimeter was broken and on one occasion the hospital was over run and all the doctors, nurses and patients were killed by the Japanese. A similar display of barbarity took place at the strip at Bawli Bazaar where two hundred wounded were laid out at the side of the strip waiting for us to land and fly them out. The Japanese attacked, took the strip and before it was recaptured in a counterattack murdered all the injured and their attendants.

BURMA

HAVING READ NUMEROUS books about the war in Burma, the Arakan Campaign and in particular about the Battle of the Box I have deliberately used extracts from those works to ensure accuracy where possible with permission. What I will try to do is to give an overview of matters so that it will not be too difficult to follow the story.

To fight a series of battles in Burma, as I know someone once said, meant that those involved needed not only an ability to fight with great skill and bravery but to overcome a number of hazards which individually could, to some, appear impossible. Taken collectively, success seems to be under the ambit of miraculous.

There were four main areas of difficulty which confronted the officers and men as they went into battle. These are:

1. the weather
2. the terrain
3. the general site for the dropping of supplies
4. the lack of fighting troops and equipment.

The weather in February/March 1944 was hot and smelly and as the monsoon approached it was sticky and unpleasant. When the rains arrived the roads, such as they were, became impassable and as one commentator reported, had they come three to four days earlier thousands of allied troops would have perished.

The terrain was mainly jungle and shrub in which the Japanese had great experience and were used to using trails and thickets. They also had the ability to stay quiet for long periods by night; in the day they would not only keep watch but make terrifying noises with the intention of striking fear into the minds of those on the plains who themselves had little or no cover.

The site of the Admin Box where the battle was fought was about one mile square with hills around the top and jungle and vegetation in between.

During the battle and afterwards Bunny, as you will later read, was constantly writing home, assuring Edith that he would not be beaten and definitely was coming home. I have now come to the conclusion that this was totally reckless, although I realise he was trying to give assurances to those at home. The chance of success on the evidence before and during the battle would indicate that the chances of survival were minimal.

The general site for the dropping of supplies was limited. Although the Dakotas were magnificent the accuracy of their dropping of supplies had to be of a high degree. In fact, their success was bordering on the miraculous. There was, of course, the possibility of getting supplies to the Box by using the Ngakeydauk Pass. Of course when that was closed it meant that the troops in the Box were completely cut off.

The lack of fighting troops and equipment was a serious problem. At the beginning of February when Bunny was commanding the Box he at first only had one fighting regiment, which was his own Anti-tank Regiment. The remainder of the men were, as the name suggests, the administration troops who consisted of about 8,000 administrative troops, Pioneers, Sappers, Signallers, Ordnance and Medical Units, Mule Companies and Native road builders. They were joined later by the Royal West Yorks and the Gurkhas. Later, the KOSBs and Punjabis were brought in as reinforcement.

The book *The Campaign in Burma* issued by HM Stationary Office says:

'Visibility during the misty days was about fifteen yards, less in the moonless nights. The experience of a jemandar of the Bombay Grenadiers is typical. Two Japanese leapt down into his trench. He shot the first, who fell on him. The second, reaching round the corpse, tried to strangle him. The jemandar shouted for somebody to throw a grenade into the trench, and a soldier

obliged. The grenade killed the Japanese and the jemandar
survived. These desperate days were, indeed, a soldiers' battle.
While it raged, all in the Box were fighting men, and signallers,
sappers, clerks and cooks seized the rifle and used it like veterans.

The Box was set in a cupped area of dried-up paddy-fields
roughly a mile square. Nature had not designed it for a fortress.
In the midst rose a solitary mound three hundred feet high known
as Ammunition Hill, but the whole area was dominated by a ring
of hills. None of these was held by our troops, for the sufficient
reason that we had not the strength available. Each unit made
itself responsible for its own perimeter, linking up with its
neighbour whenever it could. The tanks and guns formed a
protection for headquarters, hospitals and 'soft' vehicles. In time
the various sectors of the Box ringed themselves as far as possible
with wire. Brigadier G.C. Evans, D.S.O., who took over the
general defence of the Box, created a garrison equal to the
emergency. From Mountbatten came a message telling the
garrison that he had directed immediate reinforcements towards
them. 'Pending their arrival,' added Mountbatten, 'it is imperative
that every man remains at his post and fights to the end.'

What I have discovered amongst the papers is an article by
'an Infantry Officer' which I was intending to summarise but having
re-read it, decided that is would be better, in my view, to include it
as it was printed. I have no doubt that the reference to the defence
of the ammo dump with a spade is Bunny and can be confirmed
by conversation which Sheila had with Sir Derek Hodgson. Derek
became a High Court Judge after the war and Sheila and I were
privileged to be invited to dine at the Judges' Lodgings in
Birmingham whilst he was on Circuit. Sheila asked Sir Derek what
it was really like and how he would assess the part that Bunny
played in it. He thought for a moment and said, 'So far as the war is
concerned, ninety percent was completely boring and the other ten
percent absolutely terrifying.' He continued, 'So far as your father-

30. Bunny seated in centre;
Derek Hodgson on the front row, right hand side

in-law is concerned, as you probably will already have discovered, he is completely mad.' He then told Sheila of the occasion when the Japanese started shelling the ammo dump which started to cause a series of explosions. Bunny rushed towards it shouting 'Come on, Hodgson' and, reluctantly, we saved as much ammunition as we could. Bunny was wounded but was soon back for more.

SPECIAL ORDER OF THE DAY by
LT.-GENERAL W.J. SLIM CB, CBE.,DSO.,MC.
General Officer Commanding-in-Chief,
Fourteenth Army.

ADDRESSED TO THE 7TH INDIAN DIVISION.

In my last Order of the Day I told you you had defeated the Jap armies opposing you and that it remained to destroy them. The extent to which you have done that is shown by the fifty thousand Japanese left dead on the soil of India and Northern Burma, the great quantities of guns and equipment you have captured, the prisoners you have taken, the advances you have made, and the flight of the remnants you are still pursuing.

To the 15 Corps in the Arakan fell the unique honour of being the first British Indian formation to hold, break and decisively hurl back a major Japanese offensive. Theirs was an example of tenacity and courage which inspired the whole Army. The 4 Corps met the main weight of the Japanese Assam offensive, and, in one of the hardest fought and longest battles of the war, shattered it. 33 Corps in their brilliant offensive from the North not only drove a large Japanese force from what should have been an impregnable position, but destroyed it. Together the 4th and 33rd Corps have swept the enemy out of India.

The troops of 2.2, and 404 L.of C. Areas, not only by their gallantry and steadfastness in action, but by their tireless devotion behind the immediate front made a contribution essential to victory.

What you owe to our comrades in the Allied Air Forces I need not remind you. Our whole plan of battle was based on their support. There would have been no success had they failed us. Their share in our combined victory was magnificent and historic.

There is not a division or brigade in the Fourteenth Army which has not proved its superiority over the enemy and knows it.

You of the 7th Indian Division have earned a name for yourselves equal to that of the most famous Indian Divisions. Your magnificent fight in the Arakan during the first Japanese offensive will be one of the most glorious pages in the history of the whole war, while your part in the battle of Kohima and the subsequent pursuit added fresh laurels.

To the officers and men of the 7th Indian Division I send my congratulations. The Fourteenth Army has inflicted on the Japanese the greatest defeat his Army has as yet suffered. He is

busily trying to build up again and reinforce his broken divisions.
He will fight again and viciously, but we have paid him something
of what we owe. There still remains the interest. He will get it!

sd. W.J. Slim, Lieut-General, Field.
General Officer Commanding-in-Chief
31 August 44

TO COLONEL COLE R.A.

Old King Cole was a merry old soul
And a merry old soul was he
He called for his maps
He called for his roll
He called for his officers three.

Now the Division came back
And the Jap attacked
And the Colonel laughed with glee
For he had positioned the Division
As the Jap could see.

Now every artillery man
Had a small arm
And a jolly fine small arm had he
Now 'shoot' said the Colonel
'shoot the Japs with me.'

Now maps were plotted
And equipment dotted
All over the Admin Box
Jap snipers sniped as well they might
And cunning as a fox.
Now Ammunition Hill was hit

We nearly had a fit
And Jappy laughed outright
But the tanks stood fast
And the Japs did blast
And the West Yorks fought with might.

Now Old King Cole is a merry old soul is he
For the Battle was fought
And we gave them naught
But a thrashing as you can see.

As a Regiment we are proud
And our praises will be loud
Of deeds so brave and true
And Admin Box is still unlocked
And 'Sir' thanks be to you!

Sir - May I submit this to SEAC
I am Sir,
Your obedient servant
791670 BQMS
Baxter W.G.

THE END OF QUARTER SESSIONS

THE COURTS ACT 1971 abolished Assizes and Quarter Sessions and substituted, therefore, Crown Courts. As the senior advocate in Oxford Bunny was asked to undertake (and readily accepted) the honour of making the final speech on behalf of solicitors at the final sitting of the Oxford City Quarter Sessions in Number 1 Court in The Town Hall. I was his junior on that occasion. Brian Gibbens (the Recorder) knew us both well. He was rather emotionally disturbed by the occasion and was rather anxious about his own position.

He was a very popular Recorder of the City as he would readily accept invitations to attend and speak at local events. There was a problem as to who would be the new Recorder and, if my memory serves me correctly, the interpretation of the Courts Act was amended, which would have enabled him to carry on. At the time everybody thought he had to go but only to comply with the Act. Bunny's speech was made in the presence of the Recorder and the Lord Mayor and he said:

> *My Lord Mayor, Mr. Recorder, I am very happy indeed to speak on behalf of the solicitors of Oxford who have practised before you.*
>
> *It is sad for all of us that tradition should have to be dispelled on occasions and we can only hope that it is for the common good that this tradition of six hundred years has been dispelled in this case. No-one who has experienced the wisdom and courtesy which you have always displayed in your office could do other than wish you well in your new office, though regretting that it is not as Recorder of the City of Oxford.*

I have been in this Court for something like forty-eight years and I remember well when assisting my master, Andrew Walsh, at a trial in the defence of a notorious burglar appearing here when the then Recorder, Sir Roland Ackland, was very careful to tell the jury that the first count of twelve against this particular man must be recorded as a decision of not guilty. On the other eleven counts he was clearly guilty. It was one of those old cases where it was a fair cop and jemmies and skeleton keys were slung round the accused when he was arrested. Unfortunately, I do not know whether it was my fault or the then Recorder's but to our joint astonishment the jury came back and found the prisoner not guilty on all twelve counts. There was a hush in the Court and the Recorder discharged the prisoner and the jury and sat back. But really that was not the end of it all because the foreman of the jury said 'Sir, there is one question we want to ask you. We want to know how these burglars get hold of all these housebreaking implements.' The reply came very quickly; the then Recorder said 'I don't know, I have never been in the trade.'

That was I think my first experience of Quarter Sessions and since then we do not appear before you as advocates but we do appear before you as solicitors through Counsel and we are pleased to do so. I am here today supported by my 'Junior' and he agrees with me that we are quite happily prepared to leave the actual conduct of the cases to our brothers at the Bar and we are sure that that is a good thing.

Mr Recorder, I will only say one thing more and that is that you retire from the office of Recorder of the City of Oxford with the goodwill of the solicitors who practise here.

BUNNY – TRIAL OF SEYMOUR

HAVING BEEN ADMITTED Bunny quickly acquired a reputation as an advocate; working as he did for Horace Fisher, firstly as an assistant and later as a partner, he had every opportunity to go into court, which he did. He became involved in some of the local murder cases – the most important of which was the defence of a man called Seymour for the murder of Mrs Annie Kempson, who was fifty-eight years of age at the time of her death in August 1931. She lived in St Clement's Oxford. A lady friend was expecting Mrs Kempson to visit her over what was the bank holiday weekend, but she never arrived. Her dead body was discovered in her house and the police were informed. The police arranged for the eminent pathologist, Sir Bernard Spilsbury, to attend the scene and later to perform a post mortem examination. Mrs Kempson seemed to have been hit about the head with a blunt instrument such as a hammer and thereafter her carotid artery was severed, causing her death. It was accepted that Seymour was in Oxford on the day of the murder and had been seen with a hammer and the blade of a chisel in a parcel which he had with him. However, no chisel was ever found. The prosecution case in essence depended upon the linking of the hammer to the killing.

Sir Bernard was on holiday in Cornwall at the time that he concluded his report on the post mortem. He told the police that the surfaces of the head of the hammer were all too small to have produced the fractures of the skull and he said, 'I am bound to conclude that this was not the weapon used.' The police were unhappy with the opinion and asked Sir Bernard to return to Oxford for a further conference. As a result of this it seems that Sir Bernard had been persuaded to carry out further tests with a hammer on a piece of wooden board. He in effect had changed his mind as he later concluded, as he told the jury, 'In my opinion, the fractures (to the skull) could not have been caused by this hammer in this condition.'

The book written by Andrew Rose *Lethal Witness: Sir Bernard Spilsbury, Honorary Pathologist* (published by Sutton Publishing) describes the changes and the committal proceedings when Sir Bernard gave evidence and changed his mind. He said that he had experimented by putting paper and cloth around the hammer when it was possible to cause a dent similar to the dimensions of the fractures.

Andrew Rose continues:

> *Even at this early stage the defence challenged Spilsbury's modus operandi. Seymour was represented by a very young but bold solicitor R.B. Cole. 'Are you going to give credence to suppositions like that?' he asked the Bench. But the Magistrates, no doubt suitably impressed by the great pathologist's performance, committed Seymour for trial at Oxford Assizes.'*

Bunny had made a submission of no case to answer. The issues were in the open and many advocates would have formed a view that it was worth a submission, although very few would have expected the defendant to be discharged.

Bunny did, in fact, talk about the case over the years and it quite obviously had made a marked impression on him. Despite Bunny's efforts and those of W.G. Earengay (Counsel for the defence) Seymour was convicted and on 10 December 1931 he was hanged at Oxford Prison.

Years ago I remember being shown a copy of the 'calendar of cases being held at the Assizes' which Bunny had got Seymour to sign; under the entry for 'sentence' the entry was 'death'.

I am grateful to Graham Osborn-King for the information about Sir Bernard and this case which he gave to my brother, John, recently not knowing that I was writing this book. He describes in a letter the excerpts which he has taken from Andrew Rose's book and says:

In its brief few printed words he encapsulates the fire that burnt within him (Bunny) as an advocate and human being. By the time I knew him that fire had somewhat abated but I dare say that those with him in the Admin Box – wherever – had good reason later to appreciate it. Indeed I can still see him with that twinkle and ability to say 'herumph' with perfect timing as befitted every occasion. I rather suspect that anyone who went up against him gave up all hope and I know that Eric Church often told me that he only wished he could melt the Bench as easily as Bunny had done.

Graham Osborn-King continues:

Bunny and I were opening some late post with Madge Steele in the corner behind her trusty ultra-modern courier type yellow manual typewriter. I chanced to look out of the window and it so happened that a male streaker was running past the office in George Street. I told Bunny what I had just seen as the man ran round the corner towards Taphouses. Bunny smiled that benign 'tell your father' look and asked quite rightly of me, 'What did he look like?' As I recall to my everlasting amusement I replied as a child: 'Well, he was well built'. With not the slightest shade of cockiness or realisation of the inanity of the question or, indeed, the reply. Bunny duly humpfed and we carried on with the letter opening. As a reflection as to how much serendipity plays in the roads taken there is no better example of a four minute (tops) meeting with Bunny, alongside Tony Hughes and Bryn Howell Price, all just qualified and sporting long trousers. After Bunny's humpfing and smiles he leaned back in his chair and playing with his pen and looked at us with his cheshire cat smile (the one he greeted the whole of Oxford with as he strolled down Cornmarket

Street to the Frewen Club). That day he taught me about decision making, the serendipity of life, and one liners all in one go. He enquired benignly of the three of us, trembling slightly in his presence: 'Which of you has got a fountain pen?' Well, I hadn't but before I could utter a mutter, young Tony Hughes said, 'Sir, I have', and proceeded to brandish proudly a Parker fountain pen which Bunny proceeded to inspect; upon completion of his inspection of this pen he uttered the immortal line which I will take to my grave as mastery of teaching: 'Good for you, Anthony, you can go and open our new branch office at Carterton. We need someone to sign the cheques.'

So there it was done and dusted. Tony did indeed go to Carterton and became a specialist in domestic conveyancing. All such memories were revived the other night as I was reading the biography of Bernard Spilsbury. Bunny was mentioned as 'a young but bold advocate prepared to question seriously the logic and prick the pronouncement of a man quite cocksure of his own opinions. That takes guts, verve and confidence.'

BUNNY – SOLICITOR AFTER THE WAR

BUNNY MUST HAVE REALISED how lucky he was to have survived the war. He was anxious to help in any way he could to rebuild the country. Although there had been talk of moving lock stock and barrel to Tanganyika the lure of his roots in England was very strong. Although he did not actually use the phrase he clearly had a mission. He had many interests. His real love was sport and particularly cricket and rugby so that the Oxford Sports Club was the ideal fund for his energies.

Before the war he had played both sports but his eyesight was not very good and he recognised his weakness. He continued to play cricket and had to play with the aid of spectacles. As he confessed he was not able to throw a cricket ball properly so kept wicket in the hope that he would not be a liability in the field. He did play for the county on three occasions and his hope was to win his county cap. This he failed to do. He loved his cricket and had some great cricketing friends who remained as such for the rest of their joint lives.

Perhaps the best example was Charlie Walters who not only played cricket for Oxford City and for Oxfordshire but had the honour of getting an FA Cup Winners' Medal in 1921 when he played centre half for Tottenham Hotspur. I was told that Spurs were leading with just a few minutes to go by the odd goal. They were being put under extreme pressure. It seemed that if they could hold out the last few minutes they would have won but if the other side was to level the scores extra time would be played and Spurs would not be able to hold out.

In the final few seconds the opposition centre forward burst through and blasted a shot at the goal. Charlie was standing in the goal mouth and the ball hit him in the face and bounced out of danger. The final whistle was blown. Charlie was the hero but he did not confess until later that he had not actually seen the ball although he certainly felt it. It was, he said, the best pain that he had ever experienced. Although Charlie was a friend of my parents he was also a friend of the family and in the summer of 1962 together with his wife Gladys, Leslie and Connie Carter, Bernard Cole, John Cole and myself and Sheila we went to Spain, having hired a villa at San Antonio near Palamos on the Costa Brava. Leslie Carter was another great Minor Counties stalwart and, like Charlie, preferred to be taking exercise (to the pub and back) rather than make use of the splendid beaches. Their usual modus operandi was to leave the villa and go to the nearest bar to have a couple of pints before lunch. They decided to use different bars and on one occasion found a bar which was constructed of sheets of corrugated tin. They were a little apprehensive but persisted in going in and there found an adequate bar inside. As they went to the counter the bar owner let out a whoop of delight and shouted 'Footballer'. He had seen the cup winners' medal attached to Charlie's watch chain. They were made so welcome that they did not visit any other bar during our stay.

31. Cole family, Christmas 1951
Left to right back: Bunny, Maurice, Jack, Bernard
Left to right front: Margie, Bessie, Dorothy, Phyllis

115

R.R.B.C. (ME) JOINS COLE & COLE

I JOINED THE FIRM in 1954. Bunny taught me a lot about advocacy but he did not encourage me to go and see him in action, although I did on a number of occasions. The Assizes were different; they were the opportunity to see the advocates and Judges in action and to listen to their beautiful speeches which were made when addressing the jury or summing up the case. We were told that we would probably be stopped from entering the court but we should persist and take with us a file of papers so that when our entry was questioned we could say 'instructions to counsel' and move on. This ruse only failed me on one occasion but normally it worked a treat.

In my early days I had the privilege of listening to Norman Birkett QC in Aylesbury where he sat as Chairman of Bucks Quarter Sessions. He had exactly the right word for everything, spoken with his beautiful, melodious voice.

Another great advocate (who later became a High Court Judge) was Kenneth Jones QC. I was fortunate to brief him on many occasions and if the case seemed to be going down he was the best chance of setting it up again. He was a real terrier and much feared by other advocates. I do remember one occasion when I was briefed to represent the local hunt in the Midlands at an inquest when my instructions were totally inadequate and it was really a question of doing what I could to avoid any publicity and to ensure that the hunt was not criticised for their arrangements. As I arrived in good time I was horrified to see Kenneth Jones walking down the street towards me. I assumed – as it turned out, wrongly – that he had come to oppose me and, in fact, he was nothing to do with the case at all.

MAURICE BUXTON COLE

MAURICE, THE THIRD SON of Oswald and Emma, was born on 28 November 1901 in Oxford. He married Betty Buckingham and they had two sons, Roger and Nicholas. Maurice died on 11 November 1969. Having had a coronary thrombosis he had retired from Cole & Cole Solicitors in 1966 and moved to Seaford in Sussex. He was allowed to play nine holes of golf on a regular basis and had gone out to play with a friend when he collapsed and died on the first tee. He had been born at Ebor House in Blue Boar Street.

He was educated at Bedford House and was then articled to Andrew Walsh. When he qualified in 1926 he went to Liverpool and Wetherby to gain experience but returned to the south to practise for eight years in Reading. He returned to Oxford in 1936.

In February 1941 he joined the RAF VR and was posted to the Air Ministry for security work. He ended the war with the rank of Squadron Leader.

As a young man he was a keen cricketer and hockey player. He was the first President of the Adastral Sports Club and a Past President of the Bury Knowle Club. He also supported Bunny in the formation of the Oxford Sports Club.

He joined Bunny after the Second World War in the setting up of the firm of Cole & Cole, firstly in Turl Street, and then in St George's mansions.

Maurice was one of my godfathers and, as such, helped me enormously during my articles and later for six years as one of his partners in the firm. He was a man who much preferred to prosecute, whereas Bunny favoured defending. This was very useful as they built up the firm together. I did not have any preference and was able to fit in firstly with Francis Lewis and Eric Church and later with Brian McGhie as partners in the firm.

Cases for the prosecution in those days were very hard to come by and advocates were chosen by the police on the basis of performances in court. If you did a case badly or the police thought you did you would not be given another case for some considerable time. Furthermore, if you had agreed to prosecute you had to do so and the fact that you were in another case in another part of the country was not always an acceptable excuse. The police might agree to a particular case being dealt with by someone else but suffice it to say it was difficult.

A case which comes to mind is when I was asked to prosecute a man from Liverpool on a charge of dangerous driving. It was a shocking piece of driving and there was dispute as to the identity of the driver. If convicted the police expected that the defendant would be sent to prison (which could happen in the 1960s).

I duly appeared with my witnesses before the Thames Magistrates. The defendant, who had been released on bail, failed to appear and a warrant was issued for his arrest without bail. The date of the hearing was fixed without reference to me and, indeed, to a date which I could not possibly manage. Helpfully, the defendant indicated whilst in custody that he would be pleading guilty. I asked Bunny if he would do the case for me. He himself had had a heart attack and had been told to take things easy. I, of course, was anxious that he should not have any strain and I prepared the speech for him to deliver to the bench, suggesting that it was a 'shocking piece of driving'. When the file was returned to me I noticed that my aggressive lines had been deleted. I was later told by the officer in the case that after the case Bunny asked the defendant, who was not represented and was not sent to prison, how he was getting back to Liverpool. The defendant had no money and said he would have to hitchhike. Bunny gave him,

I was told, a £10 note and as we were able to charge a fee for the prosecution of £15 the profit was minimal. Bunny was not only generous but was able to see good in the most surprising areas.

HONORARY DEGREE
OF MASTER OF ARTS FOR BUNNY

ON 14 DECEMBER 1974 at the University of Oxford, the Public Orator in a Congregation presented to RBC the Honorary Degree of Master of Arts. The speech, of course, was delivered in Latin and fortunately we have a copy of the English translation which reads as follows:

I have never been involved in a court case yet, but if ever I were, here is one whom I would very much like to have defending me. He possesses a remarkable knowledge of affairs as well as of the law, and might be called the 'very marrow of persuasion', so that my innocence would be proved before a Bench of Magistrates, however keen-nosed: I cannot call them 'beaked' because my Latin lexicon does not warrant the application of this adjective to persons, and the ladies who now-a-days sit on the Bench might not think it entirely felicitous. If however he were unwilling to take on my case, I'd gladly see him as my prosecutor, not that I'd entertain the slightest hope of his pulling his 'legal punches', since he is a staunch upholder of law and order, as befits the son of a former Chief Constable of this city. I would, however, be sure that he would present the evidence against me with the utmost fairness, in a manner to ensure that only the guilty got condemned and not that each and every accused should, if possible, be clapped behind bars. To round off the praises of so sound a lawyer, I would say that he is amply endowed with 'common sense' in two of the many meanings which this phrase can carry in Latin: as every schoolboy knows (or rather used to know) communia sensus *covers both 'considerateness for others' and 'soundness of practical judgment.' Thus he has a real understanding of the occasional misdemeanours of the youth, who are at the age to which, as Cicero said 'by agreement of all some latitude is allowed, provided that no one's prospects in life are damaged and no one's house subverted'.*

Really our young men are lucky to be able, if ever they do have a brush with the law, to call on so sagacious and humane an adviser.

Though I have not yet heard him in action in court, I have often enjoyed his oratory elsewhere on convivial occasions. After-dinner speakers are usually best advised to keep their orations short, but once this soul of geniality gets started, he has his audience so completely enthralled that everyone is fearful of the moment when he comes to a stop.

But enough of banter. We greet one of Oxford's most loyal friends, who in wartime served with great distinction as a Gunner in the Far East, while at home in peacetime he proved himself no mean sportsman: in his day he kept wicket for Oxford City and showed notable agility behind the stumps, and later was President of the County Cricket Club when in the past year it won the Minor Counties Championship. He discharges with success many other commitments: he has given much help to the Oxford Preservation Trust and is the first of our townsmen to have been made a Deputy Lieutenant. Why say more? Perhaps I may be allowed to turn to good account a long acquaintance with one so equally devoted to Town and Gown by describing him in Horace's words: you see before you 'a well-rounded character, complete in himself.

I present to you Mr. Raymond Buxton Cole, D.S.O., T.D., D.L., to be admitted to the Degree of Master of Arts, honoris causa.

32. Bunny and Edith with their children, Richard and Sheila, John and Jacky, Bunny's sisters Dorothy, Margaret and Phyllis and their grandchildren James and Alison, children of Richard and Sheila

BUNNY AND THE LOCAL PRESS

BUNNY HAD A REPORTER friend called John Owen who I have no doubt was responsible for ensuring that, when appropriate, Bunny would be interviewed by him or one of his colleagues. In 1952 Bunny was the subject in the August 22 edition of the *Oxford Times* of the article entitled 'With Camera and Pen: Impressions by David Peters', an extract of which follows:

> *Lieut.-Col. R.B.Cole, D.S.O., T.D., 'Bunny' to nearly all Oxonians, is the son of a former Chief Constable of the City and an old Bedford House schoolboy.*
>
> *After a distinguished career in India and the last Burma campaign, it was natural for him to retain his Army associations and he now commands the 480th H.A.A. Regiment R.A.(T.A.) which has two batteries at Reading and one in Oxford. Recently he was awarded his Territorial Decoration.*
>
> *This T.A. work keeps him busy, but he still devotes a good deal of time in one way and another, to sport, in all branches of which he is keenly interested. He regularly played Rugby for the Nomads until the last war: he still plays cricket with the City and has in the past played four times for the County. He didn't get a County cap, he says 'simply because I didn't deserve one.' With his capable hands it is not surprising to discover that he is a wicket-keeper.*
>
> *He is 'delighted with the success' of the Oxford Sports Club, for the idea of which he was initially responsible, and whose President he is now.*
>
> *Considering that the Southern Bypass ground was not long ago a ploughed field, he is justified in his pride at the progress that has been made. He is also President of the old-established Frewen Club.*

'Bunny' Cole is, in general conversation at least, a slow-spoken, unruffled sort of man, who takes things very much as he finds them. If he has a vague grouse, it is that he feels that more folk who have had enjoyment from sport in their younger days might 'plough back' for the sake of the youngsters coming on, what they have gained, by using their gifts for organisation and administration in sport. He believes there is still so much to be done in this sphere.

I envy him in that I discover that he and his family now live in the house originally built by my father, and where I lived for many happy years before the war. A curious coincidence.

In the 25 July 1980 edition of the *Oxford Times* there was an article where Bunny was the subject of 'Army, Sport, Law; Bunny can also waggle his ears: A portrait of Bunny Cole' by Helen Turner:

33. Bunny

Mr. Raymond Buxton Cole, known to a remarkably large number of Oxford people as 'Bunny' Cole, was born at Blue Boar Street, about one hundred yards from Carfax.

Now a vigorous seventy-six year-old, he is proud of the fact that he has lived in Oxford all his life, with the exception of six years of war service.

The army, sport and preserving the old Oxford have been his chief interests – apart from his family and his legal practice – in the course of a full career.

'I like people' he says 'and I like getting things done.'

A very efficient man of affairs is Mr. Cole, who has used his astuteness, his energy, his persuasiveness and his unrivalled local knowledge without stint in the service of the causes he cares about.

Bunny Cole – it's a family nick-name, which he sometimes likes to explain by saying 'I can waggle my ears' – remembers a much slower, more cosy Oxford than we know today. His father was the city's first Chief Constable, whose large family grew up in the house, especially built to go with the office of Chief Constable, at the same time as the new Town Hall.

As a small boy, Bunny used to ride his bicycle up to Carfax to buy sweets or a comic at one of the small shops there. On one occasion, he recalls, he became so absorbed in the latest number of 'Chums' that he walked home, leaving his bicycle propped against the kerb. But there was no need for reporting or form-filling. The bike was returned to him that evening by the local bobby.

Oxford was like that at the beginning of this century, not a cosmopolitan city, but a country town, where people knew each other.

Bunny attended Bedford House School in Walton Street, under its notable headmaster, Tommy Robinson. The school is no more, but its old boys still enjoy an annual dinner, which has been going for so long that the presidency has run full circle among the members.

Articled to the firm of Walsh and Bartram in St. Aldates, he was admitted a solicitor in May 1928. He got his first job the same day, in characteristic fashion.

'My sister was married to Andrew Walsh, and she knew Horace Fisher, another Oxford solicitor with a practice in High Street. On the day I heard that I'd passed my final exams, she met Horace in the street, and in the course of a chat, she told him my good news. At once he said tell Bunny to come along and see me, and within an hour I was offered the job of managing his office.'

Bunny Cole became a partner in Fisher's firm in the thirties, married in 1936, and then came the war.

He was one of those people who realised that war was on the way at the time of Munich, and he immediately joined the Territorials. A year later he was called up, and in September 1940 received his commission. He modestly claims that it was the rapid expansion of the Territorial Army at the beginning of the war that accounted for his rapid promotion, but it is clear that he is the sort of man who took to service life like a duck to water.

He says, 'I loved the army, having a worthwhile job to do, and above all, the comradeship.'

It was in Burma 1944, by then a Lieutenant-Colonel, that he was awarded the DSO, which he received from Lord Mountbatten.

'He made a great impression on me on the occasions we met. He was a man of enormous personality, a born leader. I was proud to be asked to give an appreciation of him for Radio Oxford after his death.'

In 1945 after exactly six years of active service, he returned home, 'with my bowler hat and cardboard box of shirts and socks.'

He fully intended to finish with the army, but any organisation which has had any experience of Bunny Cole is always unwilling to see the back of him. Pressure was applied, and, with the reduced rank of Major, he took charge of the local TA battery.

Promotion followed, and he ended up as Lt.-Colonel in command of the regiment. He received his Territorial Decoration in 1952 and, on his retirement from command, succeeded Sir John Thomson as Chairman of the Oxfordshire Territorial Association. He has also been local president of the British Legion.

He was also Deputy Lieutenant of Oxfordshire to Sir John's Lord Lieutenant, and delights in the wording of his official letter of appointment, which describes him as 'not disapproved by Her Majesty.'

After the war, Bunny started his own firm and took his brother, Maurice, into partnership.

They moved to their present office in George Street in 1951, and expanded rapidly into one of the biggest of Oxford legal businesses, with eighteen partners.

We seem to have taken a long time getting to what many people would associate first and foremost with Bunny Cole – sport. A keen cricketer and rugby player, his practical knowledge and love of sport led him to become deeply involved in the organisation and promotion of local sporting activity.

The safe hands which made him a wicket keeper who played for his county on several occasions –though he was never capped – were recognised by fellow players and committee members alike in the Oxfordshire County Cricket Club, of which he was president for many years. He handed over to the Duke of Marlborough in 1978. Oxfordshire won the county championship while he was in office, and his years of work were rewarded by a life vice-presidency.

Bunny believes that the game has improved in some ways, suffered in others, since he has known it.

'Fielding is far better than it used to be. But pressure of time does mean that it is difficult to give promising new players a proper trial, there tends to be too much playing safe' he says.

Despite a lifelong interest in cricket, it was really his association with rugby which led to what he sees as his major achievement in local sport – his work as one of the principal organisers of the Oxford Sports Club.

The club brought together cricket, rugby, hockey, tennis and archery, and flourished mightily at the new ground purchased for it on the southern bypass. This is still the home of the Oxford Rugby Club.

Amateur sport went through a difficult period post-war, and the need for active and skilful management could not always be met, with people giving their time voluntarily. Bunny Cole had the know-how, the administrative skill – and he was prepared to find the time. Only a few people who worked with him know the full measure of his achievement, but all local sportsmen are enjoying its fruits.

It was the same pattern in the care and nurture of the City he loved. Bunny Cole has been active in the Oxford Preservation Trust for many years, and has been chairman of its executive committee. He recognises that business skill, and money, are important tools for the environmentalist.

'In the Preservation Trust, our great strength is that we can buy land and property when necessary. Thanks to generous benefactors, many key areas in Oxford are kept safe in this way. This power, and constant vigilance, are what is needed to preserve an ancient city in the modern world.'

A complete list of Bunny Cole's offices and honours would, I suspect, be formidable. As we talked, he mentioned just some of them. He has been Master of the Worshipful Company of Upholders, who, in case you didn't know, are upholsterers. Not that he's ever been involved with soft furnishing, but city companies (Livery) have a way of collecting sociable, effective people. The Berks, Bucks and Oxon Law Society has – of course – had him as president, and he's also been president of the Frewen Club.

He's a great family man, whose wife is also active in local affairs – she is vice-chairman of the Nuffield Orthopaedic

Centre's League of Friends. He has two sons and a daughter and seven grandchildren.

With friends everywhere and more to do than he ever has time for, it's not surprising that Bunny Cole seems a good ten years younger than his age. Like Oxford he wears age with confidence, and his proudest boast is that – as a former Lord Mayor, Percy Bromley, said of him: 'Bunny Cole is as much a bit of Oxford as Carfax.'

34. Oxford Rugby Trial

35. Cartoon by Alan Course of Oxford Sports Club

BUNNY'S NOTES

I WAS PRIVILEGED TO see a method of destroying flies which I had never seen before nor since. I was only ten at the time but I can remember the procedure quite clearly. A shovel was made red hot on a coke brazier and then from a tin was poured a generous quantity of black disinfectant – the sort which turns white when you add water to it. The result was a ghastly gaseous cloud of thick pungent smoke which reduced every body to coughing and spitting and I think that it must have scared some of the flies away but I doubt that it was as effective as had been hoped.

Oswald was a great friend of Doctor Phelps, the Provost of Oriel, and shared sartorial incongruities with him. When Oswald said to him having seen the Provost with a straw hat on top of a morning coat and striped trousers said to him, 'Provost are you properly dressed for London?' The Provost looked at Oswald and said, 'Chief, do you think you are properly dressed for Oxford?' Oswald was wearing brown boots with his morning suit. They walked on towards the station and the Provost said, 'It doesn't matter Cole – in Oxford everybody knows us so they don't mind how we dress and in London nobody knows me so they don't mind either.'

Oswald loved the Provost's story of the Methodist Preacher who dined at Oriel and refused the port with the gratuitous observation that he would rather commit adultery. 'Who wouldn't?' said the Provost.

In those days the baths at Oriel were across the Quad from the Provost's lodgings and on his way one winter's morning to his regular cold plunge the Provost was heard in his dressing gown through chattering teeth encouraging himself: 'Be a man, Phelps; be a man.'

That reminds me as to how I nearly lost Albert Allen in the Irrawaddy in Burma. I knew Albert very well and he played soccer for Oxford City with skill but I did not know how good a swimmer he was. He assured me that he was good so I consented to take him out fishing with two other chaps on the river just by Pagan. Our method of fishing was to throw in a charge of gun cotton on a short fuse and wait for the stunned fish to come to the surface. Our first attempt was successful and probably a hundredweight of fish came to the surface. We had not planned in detail how we were going to collect the fish but all we had to do was to manoeuvre our motor boat downstream and then to dive into the river and collect what we could and throw the fish into the boat.

Everything was going reasonably well until I realised that Albert was not there and when we got into the boat we saw him on the bank some three hundred yards downstream. We fetched him back with deep relief. If he had floated downstream for another mile or so he would have been captured by the Japanese in occupied territory.

I never found out how Albert got posted to me. He suddenly without notice appeared at my tent at Kohima. He had been a real personal friend of mine in civvy street. I knew his family and Edith was a pre-war friend of Albert's wife Irene. He had become a REME Captain and was attached to my regiment.

CAPTURE OF JAPANESE SWORD AND FLAG

SHORTLY BEFORE BUNNY started to return home he told us that he had captured two Japanese Officers and had relieved one of them of his Samurai sword and the Japanese flag. He said, perhaps modestly, that the Japs had not caused any trouble and they were captured as prisoners of war and detained. Captured Japanese officers were a bit of a rarity in view of the normal Japanese fear of suffering disgrace by being captured. Perhaps the war was nearly over and they were thinking of themselves. The sword had been kept under Bunny's dresser in his lounge where it remained. When my children, James and Alison, visited on one occasion they were shown the sword and continued to use it in their general games. It was not until many years later when Sheila took it to be looked at by an arms expert who said that he had taken 'the edge off it' as it was razor sharp. Another lucky escape!

The flag was of course the white flag with the rising sun in the middle but there was also a lot of Japanese writing around the sun. Bunny was anxious to know what it said and arranged for a client of his who could read Japanese to translate. It was not easy but the client was eventually able to interpret. In essence, Bunny was told that the flag was covered with messages of good will for the success in victory of the glorious Japanese army from the children of a particular school As he returned the flag he said, 'Mr. Cole, it would be a wonderful thing if you could find it in your heart to return the flag to Japan and possibly to the area if not the school as a token of peace.'

Bunny said that he replied, 'What a good idea but I must speak to my family first.'

Bunny buzzed me on the office intercom and asked me to go and see him immediately. I went and he told me what had transpired and I said, 'Don't you ever let them have it back.' It was too early.

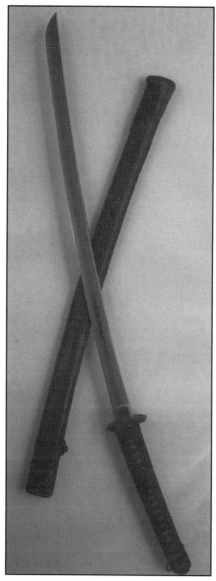

36. Samurai sword

LIFE SAVING

IN 1955 I was taken by Bunny to watch the rowing on the Isis. There was quite a crowd and what seemed like a ferry was crossing the river near to Donnington Bridge. I do not remember how it happened but the ferry became lopsided and ended up throwing a lady into the river. I think, to be fair, there was not too much depth in the water but it seemed that as soon as the woman hit the water Bunny was in the river next to her and was guiding her back to the bank. It was also quite exciting and I was sorry afterwards that I did not jump in as well. The report in the *Oxford Mail* sang Bunny's praises and he received a letter of congratulation from a man who was present at the scene. The photograph in the *Oxford Mail*

37. Life saving

showed someone in the river but Bunny maintained that it was not him. I am not an expert on photography but I think what may have happened is that the photo was printed back to front. I believe that the *Oxford Mail* would not have photographed both victims if there had been more than one. Never mind that a lady was helped out of the river and at the very least her removal reduced what would have been an anxious few moments for her. I remember going home and Edith hanging the contents of Bunny's wallet on a line in the airing cupboard.

WINIFRED DOROTHY WALSH (NÉE COLE)

DOROTHY WAS BORN on 21 July 1893 and married Andrew Walsh during the First World War. Andrew was a much esteemed, respected local solicitor and they had five daughters (Peter, Bobby, Elizabeth, Bebe and Nicky). Dorothy can be described not only as continuing the Cole blood line but forming her own dynasty. She was a very powerful woman who lived into her nineties. She was highly respected by all who knew her, family and friends alike. All five daughters married eminent husbands and have produced almost countless offspring. Fortunately, the ambit of this book will not include (except in exceptional circumstances) those further removed from the cousin status. That will be the task of someone else.

Peter was due to marry Muir Sturrock in 1938 shortly after Andrew had died. An indication of Dorothy's character was that she insisted on 'giving away' her daughter. Peter told me that Dorothy was most impressive, wearing a slim fitting black velvet dress with her daughter on her arm. Muir was a Scottish writer to the Signet (Solicitor) who served in the KOSBs during the Second World War when he won the Croix de Guerre for service in Belgium and he was also mentioned in dispatches. They had three children: Julia, David and Ursula.

Bobby married John Kell (the son of Sir Vernon Kell, the first head of MI5). They had four daughters: Caroline, Bridget, Virginia and Charlotte (now deceased).

Bebe married Jeff Jefferson (now deceased). They had two daughters: Jenny and Mo.

Elizabeth (Nup) married Pat Tipping – a New Zealander, who came over to the UK to join the RAF during the Second World War reaching the rank of Wing Commander. At the end of the war

Pat stayed in the RAF and retired in 1956. They had three sons: Andrew, Simon and Paul.

Nicky (Nicholette, now deceased), was formerly a missionary in Cambodia where she met and married Wallace Hockey, also a missionary. They had four children: Christopher, Rachel, Gordon and Anna.

DON BRADMAN

IT WAS PROBABLY 1938 when the Australian Cricket Team led by Don Bradman toured England. As was the norm in those days Test Matches were not played on Sundays, which was a rest day, and a friendly game of cricket would be set up against a local team. Bunny used to tell of an occasion when he was asked to play and to keep wicket. Charlie Walters was captaining the locals at the Witney Mills ground. The locals were fielding and one of the openers was out and Don Bradman went in to bat. He nicked it with the lightest of touches and Bunny caught the catch and appealed with relish. 'Not out,' said the umpire. There was none of the persistent yelling or pleading by the bowler as might be the case now. The decision of the umpire was accepted and the bowler proceeded to deliver the next ball.

At the end of the over Bunny was close to the umpire whom he knew well and whispered as an aside, 'He hit that, you know', to which the umpire replied, 'Of course he did but they (the crowd) have come to see him (DB) bat and not you to keep wicket.'

ROBERT MOSS

Bunny had a large number of very good and loyal clients over the years and he would be appalled that I should mention them by name unless it be with their permission or that the information was already in the public domain. Even then he would know that he could rely on me not to disclose anything which was better forgotten in the fullness of time. There are numerous clients who I would like to mention but only two that I am going to mention without fear of any professional impropriety and not in any particular order.

Robert Moss was an engineer and an inventor. He was able to make things! I remember going to his factory in Kidlington in my early days in the office and the factory consisted of six machines standing in a row, looking like six men on parade. The machines were for making plastic extrusions and the system was to put crumbs of plastic into a hopper which in turn went into part of the machine which must have been heated. I cannot remember what happened in the middle but within a very short time small, similar pieces spewed out into a basket. The ones that I saw were not much bigger than golf tees but perfectly formed in bright colours. All six machines were delivering different extrusions. How many people were needed to operate the machines I do not know but clearly there had to be someone to keep the hopper topped up and another to empty the finished article and both relied upon the skill of Robert for the bit in the middle.

Not surprisingly, the factory expanded as the profits increased dramatically. Ultimately, the company was taken over.

At some stage in its development there was a public offer of shares and it was regarded as an Oxford company which was doing well. Most people bought shares and all made a profit. I was not involved with the company at that time but I do know that Bunny became Chairman of the Board to assist Robert and his wife Madge, who were both Directors.

As I have said, Robert Moss was an inventor and as an engineer he was highly skilled. He constructed an engine in a match box and was able to make it work.

He also made his own small car in respect of which we have the photograph. The car weighed a fraction under eight cwt. The materials cost £434.00 and it took him 1,012 hours to build. He used various parts from the Mini and when the car was finished it was capable of driving at up to eighty miles per hour.

Robert was a Morgan enthusiast and he owned three of them. He wanted to build one himself which is why he designed his car as a three-wheeler and called it 'the Mosquito'. He used it regularly and not only did he enjoy driving but also he liked to be recognised as he drove this unique car. My brother John was privileged to drive it on one occasion.

38. Robert in the Moss Mosquito

The article from the *Oxford Mail* again fairly presents the case:

80 mph in a hand built fun car

It weighs a fraction under eight cwt, has rapid acceleration and a top speed of 80mph plus - and it is unique.

The car is the Moss Mosquito - and its creator is a 60-year-old Kidlington man, Mr Robert Moss. Everything about the car's appearance is unusual - even its flame-red-colour was specially prepared.

For it has been entirely designed and hand built by Mr Moss himself. And because he was able to use main components from a Mini, the cost of materials totalled only £434.

The story of the Mosquito goes back to the days before and during the Second World War when Mr Moss, the founder of the Kidlington firm of Robert Moss Ltd, now a flourishing plastic company, was a Morgan enthusiast.

He owned three of the famous three-wheelers and often thought he would like to build one himself. Last summer, on holiday in Madeira, he sketched out his design - a piece of paper which served as his 'working drawing' throughout the six months it took to build.

The design used the main components of the 848cc Mini - the engine, transmission and front sub-frame, and half of the rear suspension is fitted into the V-shaped rear.

It took exactly 1,012 hours and Mr Moss had completed his three-wheeled fun car. His wife Madge took the car on its maiden journey on roads near the factory and now both enjoy driving the little red car as a change from the Moss's first car - a Jensen Interceptor.

'The difference in the two is like the difference between wearing a sweater and a pair of flannels, and putting on a tuxedo' *says Mr Moss. 'The Jensen is a gentlemanly car - the Mosquito is a wild hectic thing - which makes everyone look and laugh.'*

It is called Mosquito because the wartime fighter-bomber was one of the few aircraft which exceeded in practice its paper specification.

And the new Mosquito has done just that. For apart from startlingly quick acceleration from the tiny 848 power unit, it has also given 70mpg fuel consumption.

'I'm tickled pink with the car' says Mr Moss. 'I enjoyed building it - everyone at the firm was so interested in the project that I felt I had to finish it - and I get a lot of fun from it now.'

Only problem with the car is one caused by the English weather - for it has no roof and to make one would spoil its looks.'

How does the Mosquito compare with the early Morgans? 'Well it is certainly a lot quicker and has much better brakes - and it is a lot stronger.' says Mr Moss.

GEORGE SILVER

ONE OF BUNNY'S SPECIAL clients was George Silver. If he had been asked to explain the relationship I am sure he would have said that George was extra-special.

He was great which did not only relate to his physical size. He was primarily a restaurateur and caterer and his enterprises in that line varied from small restaurants to fast food establishments and mobile units up and down the country under different names. Amongst those premises was a small café in St Giles, Oxford, where George established one of the first Wimpy bars in the country. In those days the premises above the café were occupied by a small hotel or lodging house called, rather grandly, the St Giles Hotel. The proprietor was Mrs Bliss. The Wimpy bar was, as one would expect, fitted out with the very latest equipment. Wimpys were very simple to make and consisted, so far as I remember, of a bread bun cut in half and toasted. On a large flat hot plate some onions and a meat circle were cooked on both sides and placed within the bun. Both the smell and the taste were terrific.

Mrs Bliss did not like the fact that the Wimpy was popular and started to complain about the premises and in particular about what she perceived to be a smell.

George hated criticism and immediately sent in experts in various fields including smell extraction.

Rigorous examination took place but no smell could be detected nor could the experts recommend any action.

After months of complaint, proceedings were started in the Oxford County Court by Mrs Bliss and the case was set down for hearing before His Honour Judge Sir Edgar Dale. We briefed Kenneth Jones QC and Leo Clark QC appeared for Mrs Bliss. The case took four days and was reported daily in *The Times* which usually also carried a picture of George. In the end, the Judge who had conducted the case in a very friendly and fair manner found that there was no smell.

If he was wrong in any matter George would accept it but if he was right or he was told so he would fight or expect us to fight on his behalf.

In my early days one of George's enterprises was the American Hot Dog Company who were served with a block of charges issued on behalf of the local authority and returnable in Stoke-on-Trent. We briefed Kenneth Jones QC again to lead this time Peter Scott (then very junior but later to become Chairman of the Bar). The prosecution based their allegations on the general premise that the hot dog vehicle was dirty. Kenneth Jones managed to get the inspector to agree that it was rust and not dirt and was able to call scientific evidence that rust was not harmful. Game, set and match – George was delighted.

One lovely story about George has nothing to do with Bunny or me. George was in Liverpool walking through the streets when he sensed that he was being followed. As a result he started to take an unusual route and was certain that his suspicions were correct. Telling the story he said:

'I went round a corner, jumped into a doorway and waited for my follower to turn the corner. When he did I grabbed him. I asked him why he was following me and told him that I was going to send for the police. He urged me not to do so as he was a film scout and had been following me because I had just the sort of physique that he wanted for their next film. He pleaded with me to attend a screen test the following day. Out of devilment I went and got the job.'

George played the part of a drug baron in *Gumshoe* with Albert Finney and later as a chef in *Murder on the Orient Express*.

Later, George joined an acting group who shared their wages equally. Sadly, he died whilst filming.

George and his wife Freda were the most generous of hosts, extending many invitations to our family which led to some wonderful 'Silver' events where we met some very interesting people.

39. Left to right: Bunny, George Silver, Lord Stone, Nicholas Tarsh, Stanley Clinton-Davies (later Lord) and Arnold Silverstone (later Lord Ashdown)

EXTRACTS FROM MILITARY BOOKS

IN THE FOLLOWING PAGES I have endeavoured to include the references made to Bunny to indicate his various roles in the battle but also to assist in giving a general view of the intensity of the conflict. The main works to which I have referred are magnificent in their detail and are well worth reading.

Of course, there were thousands of men who were under similar or greater pressure as Bunny and about whom many books have been written. Inevitably, I cannot refer to the numerous acts of individual bravery and heroism but what I have tried to do is to highlight the part that Bunny played in the changing progress of the battle.

THE DESERT AND THE JUNGLE

As will be remembered Bunny was in command of the Box until the arrival of Brigadier Evans on 6 February 1944. In his book Evans describes his arrival on page 129 and his comments set the scene for the appalling behaviour of the Japanese then and in the days to follow:

At about 11.30 a.m. I arrived at the Corps Administrative area which was later to be known as the 'Admin Box'.

It was sited in a large clearing of dried-up paddy fields and occupied an area about twelve hundred yards square. Surrounding it were high hills covered with dense jungle, so that an attacker could get right up close without being seen. In the middle of the clearing was a small scrub-covered hill, about two hundred yards in length and perhaps a hundred and fifty feet high, around which was stacked all the ammunition. In other parts of the area were big dumps of petrol and supplies, the supply echelons of the various brigades, a mule company and such installations as an officers' shop and a main dressing station. I did not know there was a hospital until the following night. The discovery was made in the most horrifying circumstances.

Since the Admin Box was likely to be attacked either from the air or by Japanese infiltration parties, the defence of the area had been entrusted to the 24th Light Anti-Tank Regiment. The Regiment was under the command of Lieutenant-Colonel R.B. Cole. I found him in his headquarters near the eastern end of the Ngakyedauk Pass.

He had, of course, earned the nickname of 'King Cole' and his outlook was similar to that monarch despite the problems with which he had to deal. He had been a solicitor in civilian life and had been with the Territorial Army for some years before the war. In the days to come he was to prove a tower of strength and he set a fine example by his energy and personal courage.

Later in his book Evans pieces together the various acts of barbarism committed by the Japs in the killing of virtually all the occupants of the hospital, regardless of whether they were doctors or patients. The Red Cross badges on their arms made no difference – they shot them all.

Lieutenant Basu was fired at at close range. He thought he was dead and when he realised that he was not he feigned death by taking the blood of a dead colleague, smeared it over his face and clothes, and thus he lived to tell the story.

In Chapter 17 of Evans' book he deals with the attack made by the Japanese whilst they occupied Artillery Hill. This was important because who ever held the Hill was able to control the battle. Evans continues:

It was clear that if the Japanese were allowed to remain in possession it would have a most serious effect on the defence of the Box as a whole. A very nasty threat to Ammunition Hill could develop.

The enemy had already made attempts to destroy the ammunition dump by air attack and by shell fire. They had twice succeeded in setting it alight. These two occasions were remarkably unpleasant. Large shells went on exploding for hours on end and the air was full of whirring fragments of different sizes which caused a number of casualties. The dry grass on which much of the motor transport stood was fired. Some of the vehicles were damaged and others had to be moved to another area and closely parked. This formed an excellent target of which the enemy guns took full advantage. Gallant attempts by individuals were made to put out the fires in the ammunition dump and it was trying to do this that King Cole was wounded. Fortunately his wounds were not sufficiently serious to put him out of action completely and he carried on though under great handicap.

Now the Japanese were almost a stone's throw from the precious ammunition – the threat was formidable.

SPEARHEAD GENERAL
By Henry Maule
Published by Odhams Press

The epic story of General Sir Frank Messervy and his men is told by Henry Maule. He deals in particular with the details of the horrific situation as existed in the Admin Box on 6 and 7 February 1944. It is only possible in this account to deal with some of the incidents which are set out so clearly in the main work.

At that time the Japanese had encircled the Admin Box and on that first morning Brigadier Evans had taken over command. When he took over, the only fighting troops available were gunners of the 24th LAA Anti-Tank Regiment, many of whom were peace-time London taxi drivers. The account continues:

They were commanded by a humorous stout hearted Oxford solicitor, Colonel R.B Cole, inevitably Old King Cole to one and all who had already prepared the nucleus of a sound defence plan. They were the only troops there not classified administrative. The administrative area at Sinzweya by the eastern entry to the Ngakyedauk Pass was really a large clearing of jungle-surrounded paddy fields. It was some 1200 yards square and British troops who fought there have since likened it to 'about the size of Wembley Stadium.' It was ringed all around with abruptly steep hills covered with jungle so dense that attackers could creep through right to the paddies' edge without being seen. In the centre was a small scrub covered hill 200 yards long and 150 feet high. There was no where, no where at all that was not within almost point blank range of any artillery, machine guns or rifles that might be brought to bear from the surrounding hills. In other words were a force to be caught within this area by a superior and resolute enemy they might well be said to be in a death trap.

There came a time when it was believed that General Frank Messervy's Headquarters had been overrun by the Japs and no one knew whether or not he had been killed or captured. The morale was low but the mood changed when he appeared, apparently cooled and unruffled and said, 'It is General Frank Messervy here. I am back in command and here are my orders.'

On page 277 of the book an incident sums up the night of horrors:

It had been dark some two hours that night with the moon-splashed jungle playing weird tricks with the taut nerves of those who watched and waited in the Box when a sudden brittle-sharp sound came from the M.D.S. Hill. It was followed by an agonised scream about two hundred yards away. Bursts of rifle and automatic fire broke out followed by screams and cries for help. The hospital had been taken over by the Japs.

The Bofors and 3.7 gunners also took toll of the Jap dive bombers and fighters that hurtled down out of the quaking sky destroying 10 aircraft.

The dive bombing was just about the most exciting thing imaginable, everything seemed to go up in the air in smoke and bangs and roars.' Recalls McCaig,'I shall never forget our Colonel King Cole strolling up at the height of an air attack just as a Zero was diving down almost vertically upon our Bofors.' Sam Parker remembers 'he stood in front one arm outstretched to stop us firing until we could actually see the Jap pilot's face clearly then he stepped aside shouted 'Fire' and we blew a wing off the Zero.'

The Japs had been so cock-sure that the British would be totally defeated within 7 days that Radio Tokyo carried on precisely according to the plan. Day by day they described the latest phase of the 'destruction of the British in the Arakan.'

General Messervy heard a Jap broadcast telling 'in blood curdling detail' of the destruction of the 7th Indian Division. The radio reported that 'most British Officers who had not been killed had fled.' Brigadier Commanders were 'cowering terror-stricken in the jungle' and the Divisional Commander 'has flown out and deserted his troops.'

Of course this was all untrue and as it later transpired the Japanese High Command was furious when it realised that they had been outwitted and ordered an immediate attack which failed.

THE CAMPAIGN IN BURMA
Published by HM Stationery Office in 1946
Page 56: The Battle of the Admin Box.

Meantime in the Admin Box none sat down to wring his hands over his fate but all set to work like men to shape it. There was gathered there a medley of about eight thousand admin troops, Pioneers, Sappers, Signallers, Ordnance and Medical Units, Mule Companies and native road builders.

The Box was set in a cupped area of dried up paddy fields roughly a mile square. Nature had not designed it for a fortress. In the midst rose a solitary mound 3 hundred feet high known as Ammunition Hill but the whole area was dominated by a ring of hills.........In time various sectors of the Box ringed themselves as far as possible with wire. From Mountbatten came a message telling the garrison that he had directed immediate reinforcements towards them. 'Pending their arrival' added Mountbatten 'It is imperative that every man remains at his post and fights to the end.'

THE BATTLE OF THE BOX
By Patrick Turnbull
Published by Ian Allan Ltd in 1979

I also wish to express my gratitude to Lieutenant Colonel R.B. (King) Cole DSO TD DL Commanding Officer of the 24th AA Regiment to begin with the only strictly speaking 'Combat' Unit in the Box who also has been kind enough to supply me with a wealth of personal detail, documents and photographs and has allowed me to reproduce the text of his broadcast made after the battle. (sadly his publishers have not now got a copy of the broadcast.)

Patrick Turnbull describes the preparations for the defence of the Box prior to Geoffrey Evans taking over command. Both Brigadier Evans when he arrived and Bunny made it clear that although everybody would have to take part in the defence there would still not be enough men available 'to form a continuous line.' This meant that they had to leave gaps. 'Between the 10th and 18th

February the fate of the Admin Box hung in the balance as attack after attack was thrown in by day and by night and the restricted area within the perimeter submitted to round the clock mortaring and shelling.'

On page 68 of his book Patrick Turnbull says:

The first of the major daylight attacks was made on the position known as Artillery Hill not because it was the emplacement of a battery or batteries but because it was defended by a detachment of Cole's Anti-Tank regiment acting as infantry. This hill dominated much of the Box's southern sector and was within 200 yards of Evans' HQ. In addition it overlooked the stacked ammunition around the base of Ammunition Hill but also the entrance to the freshly sited hospital.

On page 75:

The stocks of ammunition were another constant source of anxiety. The dumps were often hit by the shells of the 105mm gun which subjected the Box to a daily bombardment. When this happened exploding shells and whizzing small arms ammunition repeated the hazards which had created a crisis on the occasion of the first Japanese attack on this vulnerable target. Trying to put out one of the many fires which threatened to destroy the stocks in one monster blaze Lieutenant Colonel Cole, Commander of the Anti-Tank Regiment was badly wounded but nevertheless carried on till the siege ended.

THE ROSE AND THE ARROW
By G.W. Robertson
Published by Dorchester Type Setting Group Ltd in 1988

Lieutenant Colonel Cole of the 24th LAA/A Tank Regiment was placed in command of the Admin Box and under his direction all units were allocated defence areas and the Box came into being. To 136 fell the task of occupying and defending artillery and ammunition hills. These were not much more than adjacent large 'pimples' with a sparse covering of trees. Ammunition Hill took its name from the fact that it was surrounded by large stacks of boxed ammunition of all types protected from observation from the air by camouflage netting.

During the 7th Japs launched probing attacks at many places around the perimeter of the Box but their main attacks on both the east and west gate did not fall until after dark. That on the east gate was held by the determined resistance of the 4/8th Gurkhas and a detachment of 24th LAA/A Tank Regiment. In the west gate area the Japs managed to infiltrate into the position occupied by the main dressing station and during the next 24 hours they killed nearly all the wounded as well as many of the doctors and medical staff and only three were found alive when men of the 2nd West Yorkshire Regiment finally cleared the Japs out. This news spread rapidly around the Box and made it clear to all that this was to be a fight to the death. If anything it acted as a boost to morale at a time when in some quarters it was definitely sagging.

THE GOLDEN ARROW – THE STORY OF THE 7ᵀᴴ INDIAN DIVISION
By Brigadier M.R. Roberts DSO
Published by Gale & Polden Ltd in 1952

Brigadier Roberts deals with the formation of the Admin Box, the furious attack by superior numbers by the enemy, the cutting of the Pass, the isolation of the Division and the regaining of the initiative.

The fog of war had descended so thickly on the divisional area that no one knew what was going on even round the corner let alone the other side of the hill. Caught as they were widely deployed for offensive action surprised and surrounded all communications cut and their divisional headquarters overrun. It says much for the fortitude of the troops, the sound doctrine and skill of leaders and the confidence born of high morale and esprit de corps that at the end of four days it was the enemy who was beginning to have qualms as to the outcome. There were 18 more days of grim fighting in store but by the evening of the 7ᵗʰ February the Japanese had in fact shot their bolt.

They were never nearer to success than they were on the morning of the 6ᵗʰ February when at about 10 in the morning Major General Briggs commander of the 5ᵗʰ Indian Division told Brigadier Evans, Commander of the 9ᵗʰ Indian Infantry that the 7ᵗʰ Division Headquarters had been overrun, that the fate of the Commander and staff were not known and that the Corps Commander – Lieutenant General Christison wished him to take over the 7ᵗʰ Division Admin area and hold it to the last.

By this time the rain which had set in at about eight o'clock had turned the jungle tracks into glissades of mud and it was after mid-day by the time he arrived at the Admin Box, where he was met by Lieutenant-Colonel Cole of the 24ᵗʰ L.A.A./Anti-Tank

Regiment, who was in command of the administrative area, and by the second-in-command of the 25th Dragoons with a troop of tanks.

The Admin Box lay in and around an open area of dried paddy fields, surrounded by low hills 100 to 200 feet high, covered in dense evergreen jungle. The bulk of the garrison consisted of administrative units of all types – workshops, animal and mechanical transport, supply, ordnance and medical units, and stretcher-bearers. The only fighting troops immediately available were three companies of 2nd West Yorkshire Regiment, two squadrons of the 25th Dragoons (tanks), two batteries of the 24th Mountain Regiment, Indian Artillery, and portions of the 24th L.A.A./Anti-Tank Regiment, RA.

He concludes by saying,

If any unit deserves the 'Admin Box' as a battle honour it is the 24th L.A.A/Anti Tank Regiment. Not only were they ubiquitous, but they took on anything that flew or walked, and at the end of it all they could still with truth be described as 'King Cole and his Merry Men' and there is not a unit in the 7th Division that will grudge them this tribute.

(Brig. M.R. Roberts D.S.O.)

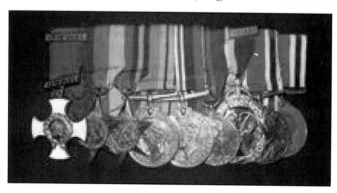

40. Bunny's medals

MARGARET LOUISA EMMA LANGLEY
(NÉE COLE)

MARGIE WAS BORN on 21 April 1906 in Oxford and married Cecil
Charles (George) Langley who was a bank manager with the
Westminster Bank. George died suddenly when Margie was still
fairly young. They had three children: Celia, Christopher (Kiff)
and Caroline. I was told that George had come to Oxford for the
first time on the day of Oswald's funeral and had been amazed by
the crowds.

Margie was a lovely lady full of grace and charm. Much of
her involvement with Bunny is dealt with earlier. The family held
her in high regard and if any member was in difficulties, especially
with children, she would always help.

THE LIFE STORY (BUNNY)

BUNNY WAS BORN in Oxford at the family home in Blue Boar Street on 3 June 1904. He was the fourth son of Oswald and Emma Cole. The house belonged to the police authority and was allocated to the Chief Constable for the better performance of his duties.

Bunny was ten when the First World War started and fourteen when it finished. He saw some of his brothers and sister go away to war and other pages will tell of such events in his own words and as to the effect that they had upon him. The purpose of this short part of the biography is to try and piece together the general picture.

He went to Bedford House School under the headmastership of Tommy Robinson who seems to have made a lasting impression.

Bunny writes his own account of his life in Oxford before, during and after the Great War but has not gone into the detail as to what must have been a financial struggle after he left school. Given the size of the family the funds coming into the house were limited and with the large number of mouths to be fed the task must have been daunting.

I do not know exactly when Bunny left school but I assume that it must have been in about 1920. Although he does not mention it I remember being told that he did factory work at Morris Motors for a time. He was also working for Andrew Walsh who was Clerk to the Magistrates. Bunny told me once of a success in the Magistrates' Clerk's office when a warrant had been issued for the arrest of a man who had not paid his fine. The man was anxious to make as much trouble as possible and arrived at the court office ten minutes before closing time on a Friday afternoon. Bunny was the only person in the office and sackfuls of coinage were piled out onto the court counter. Having confirmed that the entire amount was in coppers Bunny told the debtor that he could not accept the coin as it was not legal tender. Apparently ten pence was permitted but above that the recipient need not accept it. Bunny explained to the man that if he did not bring the cash in a legal form he would be arrested. Fortunately, Bunny was right.

Of course, if one wants to be a solicitor as Bunny did there is an enormous amount of studying to be done. It was also a very expensive operation. Firstly, articled clerks did not expect to be paid and secondly, stamp duty had to be paid to the Government of the day and the amount of stamp duty on articles of clerkship was the enormous sum of £250.00. Andrew Walsh had married Bunny's sister Dorothy, which was very fortunate for the family. They both helped him financially so that he was able to complete his articles and qualify as a solicitor in 1928. He served as a Special Constable at some stage and I expect it was after he had passed his exams. There are two medals, neither of which are dated, but they do say Raymond B. Cole and relate to the reign of George V.

Bunny was very keen on sport and he took an active part in many different kinds. He played football, rugby and cricket and was anxious to be proficient within his level. He realised that he could not reach a very high standard in some sports as his eyesight was not very good but he persisted. As an example he also realised that he could not throw very well and consequently ensured that he should keep wicket. He certainly put everything he could into the administration side of sport in later life.

My cousin, Elizabeth Tipping, one of Dorothy's daughters, writes:

> *I remember Bunny as a very favourite uncle. I loved all the Cole uncles but he was perhaps the favourite. He was fun, reliable and did things like coming and rescuing us from trees we had climbed and could not get down, playing jokes and tricks.*
>
> *Bunny was always very fond of my mother.*
>
> *When Dorothy married at nineteen she took on Andrew Walsh's two little boys from his first marriage – Francis aged nine*

and Raymond aged eleven. They were roughly the same age as her brothers (Maurice, Bunny etc) so they all played together as children. They used to play together in the police drill hall in Blue Boar Street in Oxford.

Raymond at that time was becoming interested in his later vocation to be a Catholic priest. He set up a little altar in his bedroom and made Francis and Bunny act as his altar boys. They had robes made out of sheets and took their shoes and socks off. They used to tickle the bottom of each other's feet to make each other giggle.

Dorothy felt maternal towards them and pressed for Bunny to go into the law and be articled to my father, Andrew Walsh. This would normally have cost money which they did not have so she wanted to give them a hand. The Coles were not well off as their father, Oswald, would have died by then. Emma Cole (known as Little Granny) lived in a tiny cottage in Boar's Hill Village. Jack and Bernard had gone into the police like their father and had not aspired to be lawyers.

Bunny always felt a huge fondness and gratitude to Dorothy for his career as a lawyer.

Bunny married Gladys Stroud in 1930. The marriage did not last very long and Bunny petitioned for divorce in 1936. Shortly after his decree was made absolute he married my mother, Edith Clinkard. The fact that there was a first marriage is only mentioned for completeness.

Elizabeth Tipping also writes:

I remember his first wife, Gladys, who was a singer. My father always used to say that every time she started to sing the dog howled. We loved him saying it because it was naughty. They lived in a house called Half Acre on Boar's Hill. My memory of their separation was that she left him for another man but that is only a child's memory and I am not sure.

Bunny was a very loyal and patriotic person so in the late 30s he joined the Territorial Army. During this time he married Edith whom we all loved. She was a very homely and hospitable lady. They married on 16 September, 1936.

At the outbreak of War, being a Territorial, Bunny was called up immediately and as his and Edith's home was in the country at Frilford and Richard had just been born Dorothy offered for them to come and live with us at our family home, Hothfield, on Boar's Hill.

Before the Second World War broke out Bunny had been in partnership with Horace Fisher in Oxford and had it not been for the war he would have been able to set up his practice in Oxford without difficulty. Sadly, problems developed whilst he was away which meant that there had to be a winding up of the partnership. Horace Fisher died before Bunny got home which aggravated the situation but, ultimately, the problems were settled and Bunny set up his own practice and later took his brother, Maurice, into partnership.

They rapidly built up the partnership under the style of Cole & Cole.

Before the partnership started it became necessary to put up a plate so that the public knew that 'Cole' was back and ready for business. In those days the only way of advertising as a solicitor was his nameplate which was not permitted to be too large. Goodwill was established by success in other cases. It was therefore with some trepidation that Bunny sat at his desk with Edith as his secretary waiting to see if anyone caught sight of the new nameplate outside Lincoln House in Turl Street. They used to tell of the occasion and of the moment of extreme excitement when footsteps were heard mounting the stairs. 'Great Joy' - it was Mr

Green, the local manager of the Coventry Building Society with instructions for Bunny to prepare a mortgage.

A sequel to the story was in 1962 when Sheila and I became engaged to be married and wanted to buy a house in Kidlington. We had agreed a price with the vendor and had realised that we would need a mortgage of £3,000.00. By this time I was a junior partner in the firm and hoped that I had prospects for the future. I went to see Mr Green and told him my news and that I needed to borrow this amount. I thought he was going to collapse as he said, 'I am so sorry the Society could not possibly lend you that amount of money.' He continued to say that as he knew my father he could possibly lend me up to a thousand pounds but above that he could not help.

I am happy to say that not only was I able to borrow the amount I needed within the next half hour from another building society but I have made my peace with the Coventry.

I joined the firm in 1954 and was articled to Bunny. I was admitted as a solicitor in June 1960, having started my articles in 1955. I had started with the firm at about the same time as Ronald Russell and we were expected to work hard for the benefit of the firm, and we did. We were able to appreciate the enormous amount of work which was done by Bunny, not only in the office but more particularly outside.

Maurice died in 1966 on the first tee at Seaford Golf Club.

Bunny nearly died the same year at Wembley, having stood to watch all England's matches in the football World Cup. He returned home after England had won the Cup and felt unwell. He was found to have suffered a heart attack and was admitted to hospital. Some time later I was taking out a policy of life insurance and had to attend the insurance company's doctor so that I could be examined and the doctor could decide whether I was a sensible risk. Having completed the physical examination the doctor asked if there was any mental illness within the family. I said that so far as I knew there was none. He then went on to deal with other illnesses within the family and I declared that my father had suffered a heart attack and that this had happened after he had watched all the matches. The doctor said that in his view it was mental illness and nothing to do with the heart. I got my insurance cover.

Bunny had become involved in so many other activities outside the firm that perhaps he ought to have been warned that he could damage his health. Amongst these were:

a. He was Master of the Worshipful Company of Upholders.
b. He became a Deputy Lieutenant for Oxfordshire.
c. He was President of the Oxford Sports Club.
d. President of the Frewen Club.
e. President of the Berks, Bucks & Oxon Law Society.
f. Chairman of the Oxfordshire TA Association. In 1950 Bunny was awarded the Territorial Decoration and continued his territorial work. I remember that he was constantly out 'at TA' and used to go away on camps from time to time. He obviously loved it. We have a cigarette box which is engraved as follows: '*Commanding Officer 480 HAA Regt RA(TA) May 1952-May 1955 from the Officers of the Regiment.*' I also remember being present at the Christmas Party of the TA when he was presented with a pewter mug.
g. President of the Oxfordshire County Cricket Club.

41. Bunny as President with Mrs F.M. Andrews, Mayor of Oxford

*42. The Mayor planting a shrub to commemorate
the opening of the ground*

43. Bunny planting a tree, watched by Leslie Carter

44. Bunny and Edith

45. First match and original changing rooms

Elizabeth Tipping further writes:

Later, when we went to live in New Zealand whenever we came back to England one of our ports of call was always Sunday lunch with Bunny and Edith at Southway in Headington.

They always engendered a lovely family feeling and warmth. Bunny lived life on a large scale. He was a big man and had a big heart. It fascinated my husband, Pat, that Bunny had his gin and tonic in a tankard. In fact the answer was very simple no one could see how much gin was being poured in. Edith was the perfect wife for Bunny because she was boundlessly hospitable. She seemed to have enormous energy.

Bunny liked the good life and Southway was lovely – it was big, big garden, big rooms but they were not grand.

Bunny and Edith were an expansive couple and were able to travel a lot.

They went to Australia for the Ashes and also to the West Indies to watch a Test series. In Australia they had a problem because the lift in their hotel broke down and they were on the fourteenth floor. They also had a problem when cruising, I believe, in the area of Madeira when they were struck by a violent storm. Passengers were thrown about and it must have been a terrifying experience – neither really recovered.

As I have mentioned before, Bunny's instincts relating to his military service and brought up to date by his lifesaving in the Isis led to his controlling of the passageway on his deck and assisting in the taking of women and the infirm to their cabins. He clearly had a rough time and was very ill for a long time after the voyage. The doctor explained that quite clearly his brain had been damaged and asked us to imagine having a polythene bag of tomatoes and constantly throwing them on to the floor and bruising them.

PHYLLIS ELENA GOODWIN
(WALSH NÉE COLE)

IT HAD BEEN MY INTENTION not to dwell on the history of members of the family other than Bunny but I am going to make an exception for Phyllis and then for Robert. Neither of them had children and if I do not give the background for them then future generations will not know of the great part that they played in the family.

Phyllis died on 4 July 2000. The following is an extract of the address that Sheila gave at the service for Phyllis at the Oxford Crematorium on 13 July 2000:

> *Phyllis was born in Oxford on 1 January 1909, the youngest child of Emma and Oswald Cole, born into a family of four brothers and three sisters and I am sure that there was much laughter and fun whilst she was growing up.*
>
> *It was a family that remained united for all their lives, always ready to support each other and always ready for a party.*
>
> *In 1933 Phyllis married Cecil Walsh and went to live at Seaview on the Isle of Wight; and for the next thirteen years she involved herself in life there.*
>
> *Those of us who spent many summers at Seaview in the 1970s and 1980s have always been told of the happy summers spent with Phyllis and Cecil in the early 1940s. Holidays which gave some of you your first love of the island. You will remember, I am sure, building sandcastles, fishing in the pools for prawns, swimming, tea on the beach; activities encouraged by Phyllis; and how easy it was to run down the steep hill to the beach in the morning and what a long walk uphill it was at the end of a busy day.*

Cecil died in 1946. For the next fifteen years Phyllis, with great determination, carved out an occupation for herself.

She did voluntary work for the Marriage Guidance Council and in the early 1950s she was appointed to the newly created post of The Homemaking Advisor on the national staff of the Young Women's Christian Association venues. In a newspaper interview in New Zealand in 1953 one of her quotes was that: 'Home-making is a highly-skilled occupation and one that should be learnt as conscientiously as any other.'

I only knew of this quote last week, but I wish I had known it in the early 1960s when I would visit Phyllis in London. After a day out on the town we would return to the Grays Inn flat and her first job was to go around tilting up the pictures. I once summoned up the courage to ask her about this ritual and the reply was, 'When he comes in from work Robert will think I have dusted the pictures – but of course I haven't.' An invaluable home-making tip.

In the 1950s Phyllis read for the Bar. There was a strong family connection with law: her father, Oswald, Chief Constable of Oxford; brother Jack, Chief Constable of Leicester; brother Bernard, in the Police Force; brother Maurice and brother Bunny, solicitors – who founded the Oxford firm of Cole & Cole. Cecil Walsh had been a Judge in India and his brother Andrew, who was married to Phyllis's sister Dorothy, a solicitor in Oxford. Of course, the law continues to run through these families to this day.

She became a member of Grays Inn and Richard gave her her first brief. She built up many longstanding friendships from that time.

In the 1950s it would have been a rarity for a woman to be a member of the Bar. She always retained an interest in the law and was always ready and eager to argue points through.

Phyllis married Robert (Goodwin) in 1961 at St Andrew's Church in Old Headington, Oxford with the reception at Southway, one of many family wedding parties to be held there. This was a marriage of two wonderful people, a marriage that was to last nearly thirty-nine years; a marriage of true love and great companionship.

Their first years together were at Grays Inn and then in September 1967 they came to stay with us in Burford for the first of many weekends. Phyllis always said it was the start of their love affair with the Cotswolds. A love affair that took roots in January 1971 when they bought the cottage in Taynton. From that moment they spent just about every weekend with us – our visitors' book for that time records in detail the work that was done at the cottage, and an entry in October 1971 states 'positively the last time – we camp at 35 tomorrow.' And that was their camp for over twenty eight years. A camp filled with love, with laughter, with good conversation, good food and fine wines – a home open to all of us – where a welcome was always assured.

Together, Phyllis and Robert loved to travel worldwide, but they were always delighted to be home again in the Windrush Valley. It was the countryside that Phyllis and Robert enjoyed so much. To walk in the Cotswolds or on the Malvern Hills was always a joy to them – and walk they could – eight to ten miles, sometimes more, was considered 'a good stroll.'

The last few years held many problems for Phyllis and for Robert……and when the time came for Phyllis to have special care she was so fortunate in finding that care at the Chalfont Lodge Nursing Home in Chalfont St Peter.

It is not easy to précis ninety-one years of a full life into a short space of time and I am sure that there will be things that I have not mentioned that will be particularly special to you: memories of her kindness; her sense of humour; her interest in everything; her garden; her home; her elegance; her love of animals, particularly her much loved cats; and her pottery – those items worked so carefully to record special moments in people's lives: a christening; a wedding; an achievement in a career – some of us can chart our lives through Phyllis's pottery.

But perhaps at this last moment I can draw us together in one memory....that of a visit to 35 Taynton: the enthusiasm of welcome; in winter time tea by a roaring fire; in summer time a walk in the beloved garden and tea on the lawn; and the wave goodbye from the front door – and the invitation to call again.

Phyllis loved us all, as family and as her friends, from the elderly to the very young: each individual was precious; each of us mattered to her; our joys; our sorrows; our achievements; even our failures were of concern to her and if she could help out then she always would; and she would certainly cheer us on to do better, if we could.

Robert and Sheila put Phyllis's ashes into a tributary of the River Windrush at Taynton – believing that she would want to go from the Cotswolds, float down to London and Grays Inn, float down the Channel past the Isle of Wight and on into the sunset.

ROBERT MARSHALL GOODWIN

ROBERT'S BROTHER, GODFREY, wrote the following for Robert's Memorial Service held at Taynton Parish Church on 10 April 2003:

Robert Marshall Goodwin was born in 1912 in Lisbon, where our father worked for British Electric Traction. At the age of four he announced that he wanted to be called Bill after his hero Buffalo Bill, the cowboy; and so he was known until he reverted to Robert so as not to be confused with Phyllis's cat, also known as Bill.

He was sent to England to be educated at a benign preparatory school that specialised in kindness. From there he went to Clifton, where he won the Long Penpole in 1929 and 1930, an eight mile race that was famous in its day. He also shone academically and intellectually.

He went up to Cambridge, where he was at Corpus Christi, and also spent a term at Perugia. He developed a profound appreciation of poetry and the arts. He achieved a double first and, as several letters of condolence point out, he should have become an outstanding university teacher. However, a disastrous operation when young to correct his cleft palate meant lecturing would have been difficult. Instead he brought his lively personality and creative mind to the Encyclopaedia Britannica, *where he was Deputy Editor.*

He was deeply happy in his two marriages. First to Lucy Bernstein, a refugee from Nazi Germany. During and after the war they threw themselves into the intellectual life of London, and their flat was where one could meet poets like Dylan Thomas or scholars like William Radice. Lucy died of cancer.

During Word War Two he served in the Ordnance Corps with great distinction. His colonel later told me that on one occasion a few days after armistice, Bill was ordered to take over a major German ammunition depot. This was sabotaged and set alight, but his natural foresight and leadership abilities meant he and his company controlled the exploding conflagration without losing a single man.

Field Marshal Montgomery later wrote to say that he was dismayed that no award for gallantry, not even a mention in dispatches, was permitted after the armistice. But this did not worry Captain Goodwin for what always worried him was someone in difficulties, whether from their own fault or not.

Bill was not the most religious of men but he had a strong faith in the future which is evident in the gift of his body to medical research.

When Phyllis went to Chalfont the cottage at Taynton was sold and Robert moved into Fairfield in the Banbury Road, Oxford where he continued to greet family and friends and to hold little soirees for his fellow residents. He died there on 29 March 2003.

46. Robert and Phyllis

WINDING DOWN

I AM NOT sure about dates but I do know that Bunny 'retired' on at least three occasions. His heart attack was in 1966 when he was told to take it easy (and, to be fair he did, but only for a short period of time). After his death in 1991, when we were going through his effects we found that he was a warfarin patient and there were countless letters from doctors asking him to go for a check-up which he seemed to ignore. He was obviously controlling his INR by some other means and it seems that an adjustment of his alcoholic intake may have been the secret. Warfarin, of course, is a thinner of the blood and he must have realised that he could drink a bit more and save taking the tablets. This was certainly incredibly stupid behaviour but as he had stopped driving by then perhaps there was no harm done to anyone but himself. He used to like driving and going out, particularly when he retired. He would occasionally decide for example that he would go to Lords to see a couple of hours cricket or he would drive to Simpsons in The Strand to get a new shirt. He had told me towards the end that he would rely on me to tell him when the time had come for him to give up driving. I was aware that he had had one or two near misses. However, one morning a reliable friend of mine telephoned and asked if Bunny was still driving a particular type of vehicle. There was no doubt that Bunny had been driving the vehicle in question and as the friend later told me, 'not very well'. When I spoke to Bunny later that day I reminded him of our talk about driving and he said, 'Has the time come?' to which I replied 'Yes' and he never drove again. This did not, of course, curtail his trips to Lords and with his good friend Leslie Carter he would arrange for me to take them to the Test Match on a Saturday and to get an articled clerk to do the same during the week. The articled clerks raised no objection to their training being affected and the reward was a good picnic lunch. Leslie Carter was a great friend and companion who also was mad keen on cricket and would go with Bunny to County matches in which Oxfordshire were involved for so long as he was allowed to drive. After his sight failed him Leslie would still get to the matches usually with Bunny and such was his knowledge of the game that although he could not see the ball he could follow the game by the stroke of the batsman which was, he said, a little blurred but aided by the sound of the ball on bat he could tell where it was going and he was invariably right.

Of all the activities with which Bunny was involved in later life I suspect that his presidency of the Oxfordshire Sports Club was perhaps the most taxing. His was the driving force although he had persuaded many others to help him. The administration was a great burden and when I saw him after his heart attack I told him that he would have to give up his major part in the running of the Club. He agreed, seemingly with relief, and to be fair others took the burden off him.

47. *Remembrance Day Parade, St Giles, Oxford, circa 1990*

48. Bunny's 80th Birthday 1984
Back left to right: Sheila, Richard, Edith, Bunny, Rosemary and John Smith
Front left to right: James, Alison, David, John Cole, Anna, Jacky, Sophie, Paul and Jenny

Some of the earlier articles give an insight as to his wish that young men and women should become involved with sport, not only in the playing but the administration. To a large extent he was able to achieve his goal but not entirely. He still had to battle with motorcycles and cinemas. He did his best.

THE WORSHIPFUL COMPANY OF UPHOLDERS

TO BE MASTER OF THE company and to be a Freeman of the City of London is a great honour and having been Master myself some twenty years later I know how it feels.

Neither Bunny nor I had any previous experience of the upholstery trade but at the time of Bunny's Mastership in 1972 it was not essential. Teddy Graham (a military man) persuaded Bunny to join the Livery just after the war and he jumped at the chance and made regular forays to London for Court meetings and dinners. Nowadays there is much more contact with the trade and when I was Master (1993/4) I met so many wonderful people who were amongst the finest upholsterers in the land.

49. Bunny (as Master) on Ladies Night of the Worshipful Company of Upholders with Edith

DEPUTY LIEUTENANT

On 9 April 1964 Bunny was appointed by Colonel John Thomson, the Lord Lieutenant for the County of Oxfordshire, as one of his Deputy Lieutenants. This was an appointment under the Militia Act 1882 as amended by the Deputy Lieutenants' Act 1918. The citation confirms that Lord Lieutenants of Counties are empowered and authorised to appoint such persons as they shall think fit living within their respective counties and who have been shown to the satisfaction of the Secretary of State to have rendered worthy service as members of or in a civil capacity or in connection with Her Majesty's Naval, Military or Air Forces to be a Deputy Lieutenant, such a person having been first certified and not disapproved of by Her Majesty.

Bunny was thrilled by the appointment. The events which he attended involved, as I remember, many military parades and I suspect involved his close connection with the British Legion, the Territorial Army Association and Poppy Day Appeals.

I was honoured in 2000 to be similarly appointed as a Deputy Lieutenant for the County of Warwick and I know that Bunny would have been delighted if not amazed at my appointment.

OXFORDSHIRE COUNTY CRICKET CLUB

BUNNY WAS HONOURED to be made President of the Club. I suspect that when he was appointed he was merely a name and no one expected him to be as deeply involved as he was. He did what he could to carry out his duties to the full. He would ensure that when possible he would attend every home match. He would also attend on a daily basis matches with neighbouring counties and when the county was on tour he would be with them and throwing the occasional party for the benefit of the club. Of course, his most exciting occasion was the winning of the Minor Counties Trophy in 1979. He took enormous pride in the victory and the fact that the team presented him with a silver salver which carries the inscription:

Presented to R.B. Cole DSO TD DL in appreciation of services rendered to Oxfordshire County C.C. 1979

is evidence of what they thought of him.

Bunny's love of cricket and of the county in particular meant that he was usually to be found at some cricket ground or other during the summer months. Such grounds ranged from Lords and The Oval to various village greens within the county. He was an Oxford City Grey, which meant that he would be one of a number who would assemble together on, I believe, Tuesday evenings to play the locals. All members wore grey flannel trousers (hence 'Greys') and each side would play twenty overs, with the exception of the wicket keeper each player would bowl two overs each and the batsman had to retire when he reached twenty.

After the game the members would all adjourn to the nearest hostelry where they entertained the other side with lashings of beer together with cheese, pickled onions and pork pies. After the food had been eaten, 'court' was then held under the chairmanship of Charlie Walters whose 'grey' name was Guvnor and everyone was referred to by his own 'grey' name. RBC was known as Buck; Leslie Carter as Pills (Carter's Little Liver Pills); Charles Woodhouse as Chips (he was a Master at the Dragon School). The Guvnor would hear the cases for the prosecution and would arrange for someone to represent the defendant. The charges had to relate to the game itself and, for example, Chips would say, 'I prosecute Pills for showing off in that he bowled two batsmen with consecutive balls.' His defence would be that he had not intended to take the second wicket and this was caused by accident. If found guilty the offending bowler would pay a small fine. All would ultimately become involved and hence the Club's finances were improved.

50. Oxford City Greys

51. *Sir John Masterman, Bill Miller, Lou Frewer, Bunny and Jimmy Smith on the occasion of Oxfordshire winning the 1979 Minor Counties Championship*

52. *The cup being presented to Dennis Banton by Colonel Morrell with Bunny in the middle*

HAVE ANOTHER DEPTH CHARGE
(BY CHRISTOPHER SMYTH)

BUNNY WAS UNDOUBTEDLY a forward thinking, yet traditional, *Pater Familias* to everyone at Cole & Cole. He held values that some might regard today as old fashioned but which underpinned the ethos which we all recognised, of the firm. One of those beliefs was that every Articled Clerk who passed through the firm should receive the widest possible education.

As part of this he formed what he called 'The Driver Corps', calling for volunteer Articled Clerks to drive him to a variety of events, often in London. As one of the pioneers of this elite band it was my privilege on a couple of occasions to drive him, with Edith, to Lords, where, of course, as a member of the MCC he was often hosting a gathering of friends.

On the very first occasion I drove him it was to Lords to see a one-day Test Match between England and the West Indies in the days when they were a force to be reckoned with. It was at this event that I discovered his great sense of occasion.

To all the world we had the appearance of an expedition trekking to Everest, carrying enormous hampers from the car park, through the Grace Gate, to our seats in the Members Enclosure, attracting envious glances from other members less well equipped for the day.

We had, of course, arrived in advance of his guests – all the better to set up the feast Edith had prepared. Unpacking the lunch (enough for an expedition in the Himalayas) RB reached into one of the capacious picnic hampers we had transported from Oxford and drew out something that looked like a small nuclear weapon (in reality a large Thermos flask, the like of which I've not seen before or since.)

'Here,' he said, 'try one of these. I call them my depth-charges. I think you'll like them – it's OK they're not really very alcoholic.'

He poured some of the contents carefully into a tumbler – clear but with just a hint of colour. I took a swig, but before I could ask for the recipe for this amazing cocktail, the remaining members of the party arrived. They too were also pressed into taking a swift depth-charge before the sides took to the field.

Assisted by another depth-charge or two, the hours slipped by effortlessly – a combination of lively conversation between overs and polite applause during play for the efforts on the field.

As the day drew to a close, and with only a few overs to go, Bunny turned to me and said, 'Christopher, have another depth-charge. You've got at least an hour before you have to drive back.' The result of the Test? I don't recall: although it was important at the time it's not important now. I never did find out what went into the depth-charge!

MY FATHER

ALTHOUGH THIS IS A BOOK about my father it is inevitable that my career should become entwined with his. I started working with him as his articled clerk, then as one of his assistant solicitors and later, a partner in the firm until 1984. I believe that I probably knew him as well as anybody.

I suppose that my only difficult time was between his return to civilian life in 1945 until I was shipped off to boarding school in 1949.

I remember this post-war slot as being in part very difficult. On one occasion in the middle of Sunday lunch I was asked to get something from the larder. I went off willingly and must have pushed the door too hard which meant that I became locked inside. There was no question of panic or distress on my part but I shouted 'Help'. There was an instant reaction, which sounded like a bullock running amok. The larder door was flung open and my smiling face was turned to one of tears as I was lectured, I still think wrongly, by stories of the boy who cried wolf. My loving grandparents who were present jumped as usual to my defence. I have thought of this occasion over the years and I have no doubt that Bunny was still wound up by his army service.

On other occasions he would bend over backwards to take us on outings. On a summer morning we would be awoken by noises in the kitchen – it was Bunny with Edith helping to put together the most magnificent picnic. As soon as it was finished and we had had some breakfast we were off on an expedition. One of our favourite places was to Whipsnade Zoo or to hire a boat from Mr Beesley, the boat keeper, just upstream of The Trout. Nothing would have been said the night before as RBC would take no chances on the weather.

Bunny was delighted when I was appointed a Recorder of the Crown Court but he thought it was a far greater honour for me to have been appointed as a member of the Parole Board.

When I was sworn in as a Recorder I had to travel to Lincoln where the Presiding Judge of the Midland and Oxford Circuit (Mr Justice Swanwick) was sitting. Bunny arranged lunch for the Recorders who were being sworn in. In fact, there were only three of us. There should have been four but the fourth new Recorder could not make it as he was part heard in a case elsewhere. He was Igor Judge QC, later to become the Lord Chief Justice. The other two were Mr Philip Scorer (now deceased) and Scott Baker (now Lord Justice Scott Baker), whose father 'Scottie' Baker was a personal friend of Bunny – they having had army connections and Bunny claimed that he had sent Scottie his first brief. I remember an occasion of a Law Society dinner when Scottie was making a speech and realised that a number of solicitors present might claim the same distinction. With extreme tact he started his speech by saying how delighted he was that the solicitor who had sent him his first brief was present but he would spare his blushes by not mentioning him by name.

19 November 1984 was a particularly important date for me and my family as I was to be sworn in as a Circuit Judge. The ceremony was to take place in The House of Lords before the Lord Chancellor, Lord Hailsham. My parents joined Sheila, my wife, and Alison (my daughter) and we were to meet our son James at the Home Office where I was to dress in full robes and long bottom wig, ready to be collected by a limousine and taken to the House of Lords. Normally, a new Judge would be transported to the House of Lords from his or her Chambers. It was quite a rarity in those days for a Judge to be appointed from the solicitor ranks and difficult as solicitors did not usually have Chambers in London. Lord Windlesham, the Chairman of the Parole Board, kindly gave consent for the Home Office to be used as the starting point for the hired limo.

The first real problem, however, on 19 November was the drive from Oxford to London. As we reached the outskirts of Western Avenue the traffic increased and for a long time there was severe congestion.

Bunny was sitting in the front passenger seat and I was driving. It was a great test of the patience of a Circuit Judge to-be. We all knew that time was pressing and feared that we would not get there in time. Suddenly, there was a healthy surge of traffic near Marble Arch and my intention was to drive into Park Lane. As I proceeded to move towards Park Lane Bunny yelled 'Right'. I did not know why but in that split second I assumed that there was some reason for his shout. Almost immediately, there was another shout: 'You should have gone straight on.' I was now committed to missing Park Lane and having to give way to the accumulated traffic moving onto Marble Arch. I have always been in favour of prayer and I prayed. As the traffic stopped I saw that the gates of Marble Arch were all open and I drove in under the Arch and was able to regain my position into Park Lane. I did not realise until many years later that I had committed an offence. Reaching the Home Office was easy – we had made it!

We arrived at the House of Lords at exactly the right time. The Lord Chancellor called for me and apologised for not being fully robed but after I had taken the oath he showed me the Great Seal.

Before our meeting Bunny had told me that he had had quite a lot to do with the Lord Chancellor (Quintin Hogg as he then was) before the war in his 'Oxford Days'. Bunny added that 'He may not recognise me so do not be surprised and if you are asked to introduce me do so without reference to the fact that I know him.' During the solemn part of the swearing-in ceremony there was no sign of recognition but after I was welcomed to the Bench the Lord Chancellor asked me to introduce my family. As I started to do so he said, 'Good to see you, Bunny. Who is going to do the work for you now that this chap is going to be out of the way?'

Bunny died in 1991. He had had a good innings and many lucky escapes either on the battlefield or with his health. He lived life to the full and although there must have been occasions when he did not feel well he would never show it. He took chances with his life. He was full of humour despite his failing health.

His Honour, Christopher Oddie, wrote to me after Bunny's death as follows:

What I particularly remember is the way in which your father presented me as if I was a family friend from the age of two. It was one of those moments when I realised what it was to be part of the extended family! I had a tremendous respect for his professional ability and standing. Indeed I remember when I was an undergraduate he was brought in by Oriel to deal with some melodramatic suicide we had and somehow managed to turn away all publicity and rumour mongering by treating it himself in a way which made everyone else realise that it was a human tragedy for the deceased's family and friends that had to be dealt with with tact and dignity. In short it was not simply professional skill but a reflection of his own character which defused the situation and helped all concerned to face up to it as they should have done.

He was a marvellous man and there must have been countless people who have reason to remember him with gratitude over all the years he was in practice.

Appendices

APPENDIX I

ORDER OF THE DAY
BY
Lt-Gen Sir William Slim, K.C.B., C.B.E., D.S.O., M.C.,
General Officer Commanding-in-Cheif Fourteenth Army.

You have won the battle for Central Burma. It has been no easy triumph. You have won it against the obstacles of nature, and against a numerous, well-equipped and vicious enemy. You have earned Victory by the skill, boldness and resolution of Corps, Divisional and Brigade Commanders, and by your refusal to let difficulties, overcome you, by your grim endurance, your unquenchable fighting spirit and by your magnificent audacity.

You have advanced for hundreds of miles at - unexampled speed over mountains, through jungles, across arid plains, making your own roads, cutting your own tracks, building your own boats, and always against cunning, fanatical opposition, You have forced the heavily defended crossings of two great rivers. These crossings you carried out with meagre equipment, supplemented only by what you could make with your own hands or capture from the enemy. You have driven seven enemy divisions from long prepared positions of his own choosing, which he was ordered to hold to the last. He has fled leaving 18,000 counted corpses on the ground and over 300 guns in your hands.

Every Corps, every Division, every Brigade has played its part in this Fourteenth Army Victory. None could have done what it did without the help of the others.

Nor could there have been any victory at all without the constant, ungrudging support of the Allied Air Forces. The skill, endurance and gallantry of our comrades in the air, on which we have learnt so confidently to rely, have never failed us. It is their victory as much as ours.

Every man of the Fourteenth Army and of the Air Forces which have flown with it can be proud of his share in this battle. I cannot tell you how proud I am of the men I command. That pride is felt too in your homes, in the Britain, India, Nepal and Africa you have defended, and in the Burma you are liberating.

We have advanced far towards final victory in Burma, but we have one more stage before it is achieved. We have heard a lot about the Road to Mandalay; now we are on the Road from Mandalay. The Japanese are mustering their whole remaining strength in Burma to bar our path. When we meet them again, let us do to them what we have done before, and this time even more thoroughly.

8 April 1945

APPENDIX II

We fought the Battle of the Box - and Won!
By the Author of Infantry Officer

WHEN John woke me, I sat up and in all seriousness said... 'Have you got that line through to Delhi yet? I must have it by this afternoon...' Then straightening my gun-belt I climbed past him and dropped into the small trench that constituted our command post, to take over watch. Hour on, hour off, twenty-four hours a day for more than ten days, and one is apt to set - and say queer things, and, understanding, hear them in others without remarking.

For nearly a fortnight we had literally had our backs to the wall, and we were tired to death filthy, often terrified yet somehow supremely confident. The Japs were going all out to get footing on Indian soil, this we knew from captured plans, and we were not only stopping him we were giving him as bloody a nose as ever he has had. Twice he managed to break into the Box, and twice a handful of Yorkshiremen, supported by tanks kicked him out. We wanted him to attack, so that we might kill him the more easily.

SHEER GUTS

For months now I have been in the Arakan and I've been able to get a pretty fair picture of the worth of our men. The thing that has impressed me most is the way that they have smashed the fallacy that the Jap is a superman and become acclimatised to the remoteness of the jungle. Ever since Hong Kong fell, our ears have been filled with stories of incredible victories gained by the Japanese, and of the horrors perpetrated by them. How narrow the margin between Hate propaganda and Fear. But by sheer guts our men held the Jap and now looked on him as the brute that he is. Now we have fought him and really taken his pants down and as a result are justifiably confident in the future and in our superiority. Of course the Jap is an unpleasant animal, he knows no rules of war, save to kill the enemy. We took some prisoners and I talked to a couple. They are not human in my eyes, and they are super-human.

THEY'RE STUBBORN

But let no one run away with the idea that they are not good fighters. As infantrymen, they are stubborn, hard-marching, hard-fighting and as tough as nails. They live by the word of the manual and the pre-arranged plan and that's where we have them beat. They lack personal initiative and have nothing to compete with our secret weapon . . . common sense. For many days running the Jap walked in parties into a chaung. In their original plan the chaung was their rendezvous. The fact that we held the place had apparently not altered the situation, and so our chaps had some pretty successful shoots.

MOMENTS...

I have not been away from the battle long enough to put the happening of the past six weeks in order, but there are moments and people that stick out and are good to remember. Of all those who fought through those days, perhaps most praise should go to the doctors of the Field Ambulance. Under the most impossible conditions they worked and saved men's lives.

Once their hospital was overrun and they had to crawl through the jungle, wriggle on their bellies out of their tents, over which stood Jap sentries, to escape. Many failed to get away. They were mortared and shelled and sniped and the chaung, in which lay the hospital, was never out of range of even small arms fire. The two surgeons, unshaved, tired out, wearing blood besmeared rubber aprons, and looking for all the world like a couple of knackers, performed miracles of surgery and endurance with depleted staff and equipment. Many scores of good men owe their lives to these two.

Then there was the Yorkshire cook, who managed to produce two hot meals every day we were in the Box. One day, during a particularly sharp bout of shelling, I saw him lying on the ground protecting with his body a dozen eggs, scrounged from God knows where. And there was the Gurkha mule driver who wandered into a battle, seemingly lost. I asked him what were his worries and he told me that he was looking for some fodder for his Cutcha. We found some for him and he walked out of the flying mess, quite oblivious of it all, and only interested in his mule's feed. One morning four of us played a crazy game. The Jap was letting us have it fairly hard. Each time we heard a shell whistle, we tried to judge how close it would fall and duck accordingly. The idea being that the winner ducked last and least. So much happened. There was the colonel who would insist on trying to put out an exploding ammo dump with a spade and some sand, and when his resultant wounds had been dressed, picked up his spade and had another crack. And the silt trench that held one section...two colonels, a major, a subaltern and three Gurkhas, all mucking in. Then the officer who spent most of his days sewing buttons on people's trousers and coats.

'THINGS' AT NIGHT

There was the sensation of almost regret when The Pass was eventually opened and our immediate fate decided. The nights when one felt that death was inevitable, and all one's past flooded out to the ears of the nearest neighbour. The dragging of the eyelids, towards the end of one's sentry watch. The rum ration that came round in the early hours of the morning. The incredible 'things' one saw in the moonlight. I remember waking up John and

*getting up and getting him to verify something that I had seen...
'About sixty Japs, wiring.' That's what I thought, so I called up
the bren gunner, and he saw them too. I hate to admit it, but I let
'Them' have a burst and they turned out to be about a dozen
bamboo leaves.*

ILLUSIONS

*Then I saw my whole family sitting about ten yards in front
of me. John saw them too, only in his case they were his old school
team. I once saw a six foot Jap cleaning his teeth inside my post.
All of us suffered from these illusions, and it is a good chit for the
discipline and fire control of the troops that very few cases of
shadow shooting occurred.*

*Now it is all over, the Jap must be a very worried man. He
has, without doubt, worked out his whole offensive for this year
from China down to the Bay of Bengal on the assumption that we
would retreat when cut off. With the troops we now have, and the
wonderful support given by the RAF and the USAAF, both in
keeping the Jap out of the sky and in supplying us with food, we
need never again withdraw if threatened from the rear. Stand, and
fight, and kill, and having killed, advance against a depleted and
demoralised enemy.*

*Of all the lessons that February's fighting has taught us, this
is the most important. We have beaten the Jap at his own game,
and can go on doing it.*